Revision Questions
for
Standard Grade
Chemistry

D0993310

D. A. Buchanan
(Moray House Institute,
Heriot-Watt University)

J. R. Melrose
(Lenzie Academy,
Lenzie, Glasgow)

Editorial assistance by
J. M. Briggs
(Dalziel High School, Motherwell)

Published by
Chemcord
16 Inch Keith
East Kilbride
Glasgow

ISBN   1 870570 64 2

© Buchanan & Melrose , 1997

Typeset by J.M. Briggs

Printed by Bell and Bain Ltd, Glasgow

Contents

Topics

Note to teachers

The exercises are specifically written to test students' understanding of the key ideas in the Standard Grade Chemistry course and to give students practice in the kinds of question used in the examinations. They have been trialled over a number of years and found to be an invaluable revision aid.

The questions cover both Knowledge and Understanding and Problem Solving and are classified at General and Credit Levels.

The exercises are, by and large, independent of each other and consequently they can be used to fit almost any teaching order. They can be used in a variety of situations, eg for examination revision, self-study time in school, homework, etc.

The variation in the length of the exercises is a reflection of the different kinds of questions which have been associated with a particular part of the course. Teachers may wish to focus on areas which are known to be difficult for their students.

A book of answers to the revision questions is also available.

Acknowledgement

A number of the questions in the exercises come from or have evolved from questions used in the SCE examinations. The publisher wishes to thank the Scottish Qualifications Authority for permission to use examination questions in these ways.

Topic 1   Chemical Reactions
General Level

1. (a) Explain what is meant by a chemical reaction.
    (b) In the grid, which boxes refer to a chemical reaction?

A	a puddle of water evaporating	**B**	frying an egg
C	salt dissolving in water	**D**	the burning of petrol
E	the melting of a plastic	**F**	nitrogen combining with hydrogen
G	wool growing on a sheep	**H**	the breaking of glass
I	separating alcohol from water	**J**	the rotting of compost
K	separating sand from water	**L**	heating a metal

2. In each of the following reactions, what might be seen that shows that a chemical reaction is taking place?
    (a) sodium reacting with chlorine to form sodium chloride
    (b) the burning of coal
    (c) magnesium reacting with dilute acid to form hydrogen

3. Explain what is meant by
    (a) a chemical equation,   (b) a reactant,   (c) a product.

4. Find out the name and symbol of an element which is
    (a) stored under oil,   (b) stored under water,
    (c) used as lead in pencils,   (d) used in solution in the swimming baths,
    (e) used as the metal in domestic light bulbs,   (f) used as the gas in domestic light bulbs,
    (g) once used to fill airships,   (h) now used in lighter than air balloons,

(i) makes up approx. 80% of the air, (j) makes up approx. 20% of the air,

(k) called after a planet, (l) called after a continent,

(m) called after an American state, (n) called after Albert Einstein,

(o) called after the man who discovered dynamite, (p) called after the woman who discovered radium,

(q) called after Dimitri Mendeleev, (r) called after a village in Scotland.

5. (a) Explain what is meant by

    (i) an element, (ii) a compound.

(b) Explain whether or not it is possible to make different substances by breaking up

    (i) an element, (ii) a compound.

(c) Look at the following list of substances:

iron, sodium sulphite, carbon, oxygen, sugar, salt, copper chloride, magnesium

Which can be broken up to make different substances?

6. Divide the following list of substances into elements and compounds:

carbon, petrol, alcohol, zinc, oxygen, sugar, sodium chloride, gold, copper sulphate, nitrogen, aluminium, silver oxide

7. (a) Name the compound which is formed when each of the following pairs of elements join up.

    (i) magnesium and chlorine   (ii) lead and sulphur

    (iii) sodium and oxygen   (iv) hydrogen and iodine

(b) Name **two** possible compounds containing potassium, sulphur and oxygen.

8. When iron and sulphur are mixed and heated in a test tube until the mixture glows red, the iron cannot be separated from the sulphur using a magnet.

(a) What name is given to substances like iron and sulphur which contain only one kind of atom?

(b) Why can the iron **not** be separated from the sulphur after heating?

9.

A colourless gas **W** relights a glowing splint.

W reacts with magnesium to form a white powder **X**.

W reacts with a black solid **Y** to form a colourless gas **Z**.

Z turns lime water milky.

Name the substances **W**, **X,Y** and **Z**.

10. Copy the list of substances and complete all the columns.
    (One example is already done for you.)

Formula of substance	Element	Compound	Elements present
$CaSO_3$	No	Yes	calcium, sulphur, oxygen
He			
NaBr			
LiCl			
ZnI_2			
Fe			
KNO_3			
Xe			
I_2			
$BaSO_4$			
Sn			
HCl			
Hg			
As			
$MgCO_3$			

11. Read the passage below carefully.

> Oxygen is involved in many everyday reactions.
>
> Glucose is a compound containing carbon, hydrogen and oxygen. It is built up in plants from carbon dioxide and water in a process called photosynthesis. Oxygen is released in the reaction.
>
> The starch in our food is broken down to form glucose.
> During respiration, glucose and oxygen react and energy is produced in the process.
>
> The reaction of oxygen with coal and gas releases energy which can be used as a source of heat in our houses. In a car engine, petrol combines with oxygen in another energy-producing reaction.
>
> Oxygen, as well as water, is involved in the rusting iron - a reaction which costs this country many millions of pounds each year. The iron can be protected by coating the surface with zinc, copper or gold.

Make a table to show all the elements and compounds mentioned in the passage.

12. Crude oil is a mixture of compounds.
    (a) Explain what is meant by a mixture.
    (b) Consider the following list of substances:

        air, iron, oxygen, water, milk, soil, carbon dioxide

        Make a table showing
        (i) the substances which are mixtures,
        (ii) the substances which are pure.

13. (a) Explain what is meant by
        (i) a solute,   (ii) a solvent,
        (iii) a solution.
    (b) Household vinegar is made by dissolving ethanoic acid in water.
        Name
        (i) the solute,   (ii) the solvent,
        (iii) the solution.

14. "Handwarmers" are intended for use by people who spend time in cold conditions.

    They consist of an outer packet made of strong plastic plus metal foil.

    The packet contains colourless crystals and a weak inner bag which is full of a grey powder.

    When the packet is rubbed between the hands, the inner bag breaks open and its contents mix with the crystals.

    The packet can then be placed in a pocket or glove to keep the hands warm for a period of time.

    If the packet is opened after being used it is found to contain only a black powder.

    Suggest **two** pieces of evidence from the passage to support the idea that handwarmers work by means of a chemical reaction.

15. Chlorine is used in a wide range of chemicals.

    More chlorine (27%) is used to make the plastic PVC than for any other use.

    Solvents for dry cleaning and paints require 16% of the chlorine produced.

    17% is used for making aerosol propellants.

    Chemical reactions making, for example, hydrochloric acid and bleach, account for 14% of the chlorine used.

    Other uses include the making of disinfectants, anaesthetics and insecticides (26%).

    Construct a table with two headings to show this information.

16. Black and white photographic papers can be made with different proportions of silver compounds.

There are three **types**. Here are their names and **compositions.**

bromide   (100% silver bromide)
bromo-chloride   (60% silver bromide, 40% silver chloride)
chloro-bromide   (60% silver chloride, 40% silver bromide)

Some **examples** of papers are:

Brovira and Pal - bromide papers
Galerie, Oriental and Elite - bromo-chloride
Record-Rapid and Portriga - chloro-bromide type

Choose suitable headings and present the information about **types**, **compositions** and **examples** in the form of a table.

17. On Andy's first day in chemistry his teacher demonstrated an experiment to the class. Here is the report that Andy wrote in his notebook.

> Mr. Murray took this really thin kind of copper and put it in a jar of gas. The gas was chlorine. We had to keep clear of the chlorine he said.
> When the copper went in the gas, it shrivelled up. Then it went on fire. When it stopped there was yellow stuff in the jar. This is a CHEMICAL REACTION.

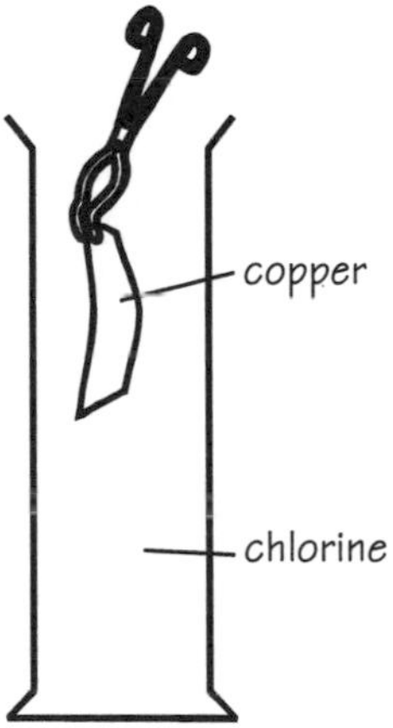

copper

chlorine

(a) From Andy's report give **two** pieces of evidence which suggest that a chemical reaction had taken place.

(b) Name the compound formed in this reaction.

18. Arctic seas support more life than might be expected. This is mainly due to the greater availability of dissolved oxygen in the colder water.

The table shows the relationship between the temperature of the water and the amount of dissolved oxygen.

Temperature of water / °C	0	20	40	60	70	80
Concentration of dissolved oxygen / grams in each cubic metre	69.4	43.4	30.8	22.7	18.6	13.8

(a) Draw a **line graph** to show these results.

(b) The average temperature of the seas around Scotland is approximately 9°C. Give the concentration of oxygen available at this temperature.

(c) Give the temperature of the water which contains 25 g of dissolved oxygen in each cubic metre.

Topic 2   Speed of Reactions
General Level

1. List the following in order of rate of reaction, fastest first:

    milk turning sour,   an egg frying,   a motor car rusting,   a match igniting

2. The speed of a reaction depends on the reaction conditions.
   Describe how each of the following affects the speed of a reaction.
   (a) particle size of the reactants
   (b) concentration of the reactants
   (c) temperature of the reactants
   (d) using a catalyst

3. Three experiments are set up as shown. Each experiment is carried out at
   room temperature and the mass of magnesium is the same in each case.

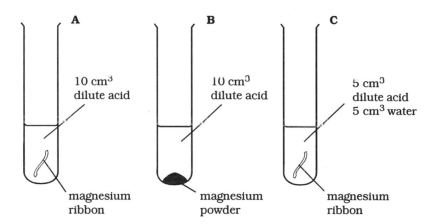

   (a) Explain any difference that would be observed between
       (i) **A** and **B**,
       (ii) **A** and **C**.
   (b) Explain any difference that would be observed if experiment **A** was
       repeated at 50 °C.

4. Natural gas will burn in a bunsen burner.
   (a) What happens to the temperature of the flame when the air hole is opened.
   (b) Explain your answer.

5. A jet of petrol is sprayed into the carburettor of a car.

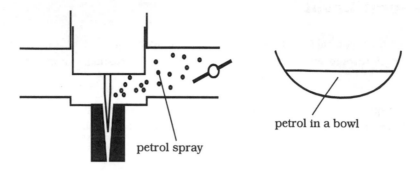

petrol spray

petrol in a bowl

Explain why the spray of petrol burns faster than the petrol in the bowl.

6. Explain each of the following.
   (a) Small sticks of wood burn faster than logs.
   (b) When bellows are used to blow air on to a fire, the fire burns brighter.
   (c) Food is preserved longer when stored in a fridge.
   (d) Plants grow faster in a green-house than in the open-air.
   (e) Large potatoes take longer to cook than small potatoes.
   (f) An oxy-acetylene flame is hot enough to cut through metal.
       The flame obtained by burning acetylene in air is not.

7. Different chemical reactions happen at different speeds.
   Give an example of an everyday reaction which
   (a) is finished after a few seconds,
   (b) takes between a few minutes and a few hours to be finished,
   (c) goes on for many years.

8. Catalysts are used in many industrial reactions,
   eg. manufacture of sulphuric acid.
   (a) Explain what is meant by a catalyst.
   (b) Explain why catalysts are used in many industrial reactions.

9. When Stephanie added manganese dioxide to hydrogen peroxide solution, oxygen was produced. Manganese dioxide is a catalyst.

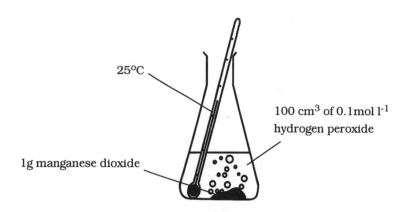

(a) What is the purpose of a catalyst?

(b) What will be the mass of manganese dioxide at the end of the experiment?

(c) Stephanie wanted to see if raising the temperature to 35°C would speed up the reaction.

Copy the diagram and label it to show how she would make her second experiment a fair test.

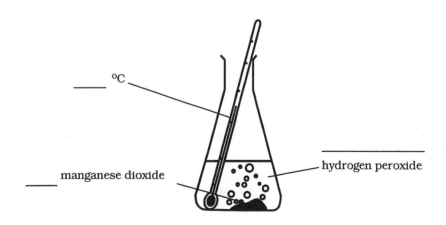

10. The graph shows the volume of carbon dioxide produced in the reaction of calcium carbonate powder with dilute hydrochloric acid.

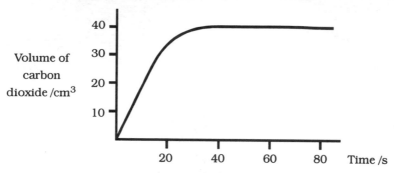

The experiment was repeated under two different conditions. For both reactions, the volume and concentration of the hydrochloric acid remained the same.

(a) What would have happened to the volume of gas produced in the first 20 s when the temperature was increased?

(b) What would have been the final volume of gas produced when the same mass of calcium carbonate lumps was used?

11. Mary was investigating the reaction of marble chips with excess dilute hydrochloric acid. Her results for two experiments are shown below.

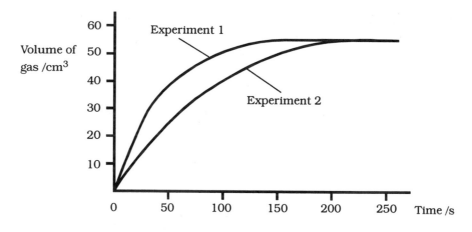

(a) What volume of gas was produced in Experiment 1 during the first 90 s?

(b) In the initial stages, the reaction in Experiment 2 was slower than in Experiment 1.

   (i) How can this be concluded from the graph?

   (ii) Suggest **two** changes in conditions which could have resulted in the slower reaction.

(c) Mary used the same mass of marble chips in each experiment. How can this be concluded from the graph?

Topic 2

12. The graph shows the volume of hydrogen produced in the reaction of magnesium ribbon with excess dilute hydrochloric acid.

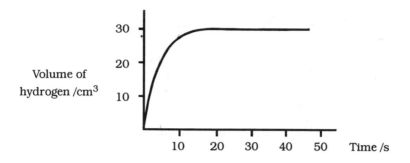

(a) State the volume of hydrogen which was produced after 10 s.

(b) State the time required to produce 20 cm^3 of hydrogen.

(c) State the total volume of hydrogen produced.

(d) Copy the graph and add a second curve to show the results that you would expect to obtain if the same mass of magnesium reacted with excess of more concentrated hydrochloric acid.

13. The graph shows the volume of carbon dioxide produced in the reaction of calcium carbonate powder and calcium carbonate lumps with excess dilute hydrochloric acid.

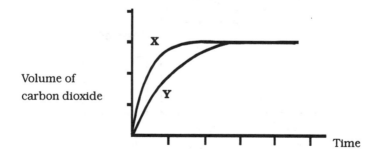

(a) Which curve, **X** or **Y**, shows the results using calcium carbonate powder?

(b) State **three** variables which must be kept the same when comparing the reactions.

14. The graph shows the volume of oxygen produced by the decomposition of hydrogen peroxide under normal conditions.

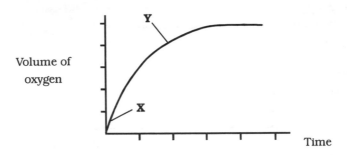

(a) Is the rate of reaction faster at **X** or **Y**?

(b) Copy the graph and add a second curve to show the results that you would expect to obtain if the experiment was repeated with the only change being the addition of a catalyst.

15. Zinc reacts with sulphuric acid to produce hydrogen.

Adding copper sulphate solution is thought to speed up the reaction.

You are given the chemicals shown in the following diagram:

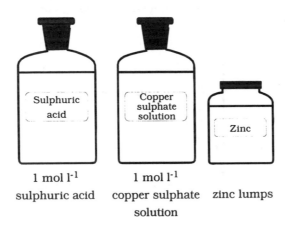

1 mol l⁻¹   1 mol l⁻¹
sulphuric acid   copper sulphate   zinc lumps
                  solution

Describe how you would investigate the effect of adding copper sulphate solution on the speed of the reaction between zinc and sulphuric acid.

16. Most polymers are insoluble in water. Some hospitals collect dirty clothing and bedding in bags made from a special polymer which dissolves in hot water. These bags can be sealed and put into washing machines. The risk of infection from touching dirty material is less.

You have been given several samples of different water-soluble polymers and have been asked to find which of them dissolves fastest in warm water.

You are given these instructions.

    1.   Pour water into beaker.

    2.   Add polymer being tested and start stopclock.

    3.   Stir once every 30 s.

    4.   When the polymer has completely dissolved, stop the clock.

It is necessary to make fair comparison of the different polymers.

State **two** factors which must be kept the same in all tests.

17. Indigestion can be caused by too much acid in the stomach.Six pupils set up experiments to find out which of two indigestion tablets dissolved in water more quickly. Three used "Calmo" tablets and three used "Easo" tablets.

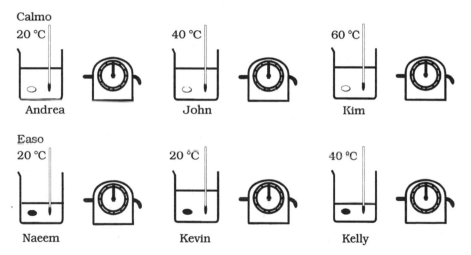

Calmo

20 °C — Andrea   40 °C — John   60 °C — Kim

Easo

20 °C — Naeem   20 °C — Kevin   40 °C — Kelly

(a) Why would Andrea's and Kevin's experiments, taken together, provide the fairest way of comparing how quickly Calmo and Easo dissolved?

(b) The results of the experiments carried out by Andrea, John and Kim can be compared.

What would this comparison show?

18. A class was asked to measure how the rate at which ice melts is affected by salt. They were provided with the following equipment:

    ice cubes in a tray   measuring cylinder   salt

        filter funnel   stopclock

Describe the steps which could be used to carry out this investigation using **all the equipment and chemicals listed above**.

19. Pauline was studying rates of reaction. She set up three experiments in which magnesium carbonate was added to equal volumes of dilute hydrochloric acid. In each experiment, some magnesium carbonate remained unreacted.

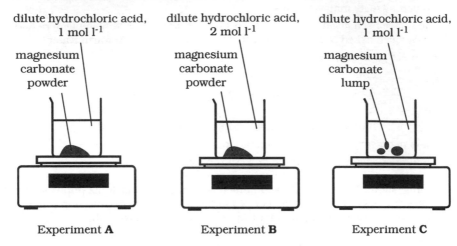

dilute hydrochloric acid, 1 mol l⁻¹
magnesium carbonate powder

dilute hydrochloric acid, 2 mol l⁻¹
magnesium carbonate powder

dilute hydrochloric acid, 1 mol l⁻¹
magnesium carbonate lump

Experiment **A**   Experiment **B**   Experiment **C**

(a) Place the experiments in order of increasing reaction rate.

(b) Pauline noted the balance readings and found that, at the end of all the experiments, the readings showed a decrease in mass.

Why was the decrease in mass twice as much in Experiment **B** as in Experiment **A**?

20. Jenny added lumps of zinc to 100 cm^3 of 2 mol l^{-1} sulphuric acid in a flask. Every two minutes she noted the mass of the flask and contents.

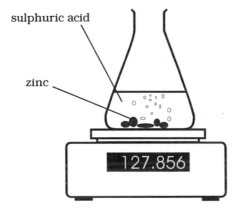

sulphuric acid

zinc

127.856

Time / min	Total mass loss / mg
0	0
2	130
4	210
6	260
8	300
10	330
12	330

(a) Draw a **line graph** of loss of mass against time.

(b) Add a dotted line to show the curve you would expect if the experiment was repeated using the same mass of powdered zinc.

(c) Why there was a loss of mass from the flask?

21. Kirsty was investigating the reaction of calcium with water. This reaction produces hydrogen gas. A solution of calcium hydroxide was also formed. Kirsty collected the hydrogen in a measuring cylinder and obtained the results shown in the table.

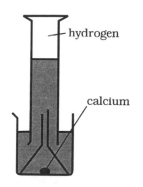

Time / min	Volume of hydrogen / cm^3
0	0
4	16
8	32
12	44
16	50
20	50

(a) Draw a **line graph** of volume of hydrogen produced against time.

(b) Use your graph to find the volume of hydrogen collected in the first two minutes of Kirsty's experiment.

(c) Suggest **one** way of speeding up the reaction.

22. A company which produces sweets was introducing a new product called "Moon Dust". This sweet was in the form of a powder which fizzed in water. The fizziness was checked before it was put on the market. Three different experiments were carried out.

Experiment	Mass of powder added to 1 litre of water / g	Temperature / °C
1	40	25
2	40	37
3	20	25

For each experiment, a graph was plotted of the volume of gas produced against time.

The graph for Experiment 1 is shown.

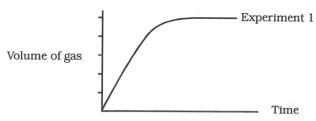

Copy the graph and draw curves to represent Experiment 2 and Experiment 3.

Topic 3 Atoms and the Periodic Table

General Level

1. Name **two** elements which are
    (a) metallic,
    (b) non - metallic,
    (c) solid at room temperature,
    (d) liquid at room temperature,
    (e) gas at room temperature,
    (f) naturally occurring as compounds,
    (g) naturally occurring as elements,
    (h) made in the lab by scientists.

2. The elements are arranged in the Periodic Table.
    Explain what is meant by
    (a) a group,
    (b) a period.

3. (a) (i) What name is given to the "core" at the centre of the atom?
        (ii) What charge has this "core"?
    (b) (i) What name is given to the particles which move around the outside of the atom?
        (ii) What charge do these particles have?
    (c) Explain why an atom is neutral.

4. (a) Name the elements with each of the following atomic numbers.
        (i) 23   (ii) 3   (iii) 18   (iv) 28
        (v) 17   (vi) 19   (vii) 10   (viii) 9
    (b) From the list above, name the elements which are members of each of the following families.
        (i) the halogens   (ii) the alkali metals
        (iii) the transition metals   (iv) the noble gases
    (c) State a chemical property of
        (i) the alkali metals,   (ii) the noble gases.

5. (a) Name the elements with each of the following electron arrangements.
        (i) 2,8,1   (ii) 2,8   (iii) 2,8,3
        (iv) 2,4   (v) 2,7   (vi) 2,8,4
    (b) Which **two** of the above elements will have similar chemical properties?

6. Consider this list of elements:
    magnesium, carbon, oxygen, chlorine, sodium, nitrogen
    (a) Which element has an atomic number of 17?
    (b) Which element has 11 electrons in each of its atoms?
    (c) Which element has atoms which have a mass of 12 amu?
    (d) Which element has an electron arrangement of 2,6?

7. State **three** ways in which magnesium atoms are different from calcium atoms.

8. Germanium is so similar to silicon that it was once called "eka silicon".
    Why are germanium and silicon similar to each other?

9.

> A lemonade bottle was made by heating
> 200 g sand with 150 g of sodium
> carbonate and 50 g of calcium carbonate.

(a) Present this information as a table. Remember to give suitable headings.

(b) Present this information in another suitable way.

(c) Sometimes colouring agents are added to glass during manufacture.
    Chromium oxide turns glass green, and cobalt oxide turns glass blue.
    Sodium oxide and calcium oxide have no effect.
    What general statement can be made about the metal elements present in
    colouring agents?

10. Some trends in the reactions of elements and their compounds can be shown on
    the Periodic Table. Here is one example which deals with the extraction of metals.

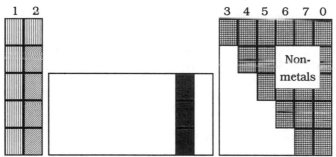

Key

Source of metal	Extraction method
Soluble compounds	Using electricity
Insoluble compounds	Using electricity
Free metals	—————————
Insoluble oxides / sulphides	Heating with carbon or carbon monoxide

(a) Using the above information and a Periodic Table in the data booklet,
    suggest an extraction method for strontium (atomic number 38).

(b) What general statement can be made about the position of a metal in the
    Periodic Table and its ease of extraction?

Credit Level

11. Copy and complete the following table.

Subatomic particle	Mass	Charge	Location in atom
electron			
proton			
neutron			

12. (a) Explain what is meant by
    (i) the atomic number,
    (ii) the mass number,
    of an atom of an element.
    (b) An atom of potassium can be written as $_y^x$K.
    State the information which is given by
    (i) x,
    (ii) y.

13. Calculate the number of protons, neutrons and electrons in each of the following atoms of elements.
    (a) $_{11}^{23}$Na
    (b) $_8^{16}$O
    (c) $_1^3$H
    (d) $_{17}^{35}$Cl
    (e) $_1^1$H
    (f) $_{20}^{40}$Ca
    (g) $_{19}^{39}$K
    (h) $_3^7$Li
    (i) $_{16}^{32}$S

14. An atom of sodium can be written as $_{11}^{23}$Na.
    Write each of the atoms below in a similar way.
    (a) An oxygen atom with 10 neutrons.
    (b) An atom, atomic number 6, with 7 neutrons.
    (c) An atom with 17 protons and 20 neutrons.
    (d) An atom of hydrogen, mass number 3.

15. Ernest Rutherford used alpha particles to find out about atomic structures.
    An alpha particle is a positive particle which can gain two electrons to become a neutral atom.
    An alpha particle has a mass number of 4 and an atomic number of 2.
    Calculate the number of protons, neutrons and electrons in an alpha particle.

16. (a) Copy and complete the following table.

Element	Atomic number	Mass number	Number of protons	Number of neutrons	Number of electrons
Ne		22			
N				7	
Ca		40			
A	4	9			
B		14			6
C		89	36		
D			10	10	
E				17	15

(b) Identify elements **A, B, C, D** and **E**.

17. Bromine has a relative atomic mass of 80.

Analysis of a sample of bromine shows that it contains two isotopes, one with a relative mass of 79 and the other with a relative mass of 81.

(a) Explain what is meant by isotopes.

(b) From the information, what can be said about the proportions of the isotopes in the sample?

18. $^{20}_{10}$Ne and $^{22}_{10}$Ne are two different kinds of neon atom.

(a) In what ways are the kinds of neon atom different?

(b) Explain why the atoms can be regarded as atoms of the same element.

(c) What further information is needed to calculate the relative atomic mass (atomic weight) of neon?

19. Normal hydrogen atoms, $^{1}_{1}$H, are known as protium atoms.

(a) (i) How many protons are there in a protium nucleus?

(ii) How many neutrons are there in a protium nucleus?

(iii) What name is given to the total number of protons and neutrons in the nucleus of an atom?

(b) Deuterium, $^{2}_{1}$H, is another type of hydrogen atom.

(i) How many protons are there in a deuterium nucleus?

(ii) How many neutrons are there in a deuterium nucleus?

(iii) Suggest why deuterium is sometimes referred to as "heavy" hydrogen.

(c) What name is given to pairs of atoms such as protium and deuterium?

20. Two types of lithium atom are $^{6}_{3}$Li and $^{7}_{3}$Li.

Lithium has a relative atomic mass of 6.9.

(a) What term is used to decribe the different types of lithium atom?

(b) What can be said about the proportions of each type of atom in lithium?

21. Atom **A** has mass number 239 and atomic number 93.

Atom **B** has a mass number 239 and atomic number 94.

(a) How many protons has **A**?

(b) How many neutrons has **B**?

(c) (i) Are atoms **A** and **B** of the same element?

(ii) Explain your answer.

22. Copper has a relative atomic mass (atomic weight) of 63.5. It contains two different kinds of atom: ^{63}Cu and ^{65}Cu

(a) How many neutrons are present in each kind of atom?

(b) Which kind of atom is more common in copper?

23. In the reactions occurring in the sun, some atoms collide with such force that their nuclei join together to make one new nucleus.

(a) Why must a new element be formed in reactions of this kind?

(b) Helium is formed in solar reactions.

Nuclei of which element join together to make helium?

24. Dimitri Mendeleev used the properties of the elements to help arrange them in his Periodic Table.

He left gaps in the table if no known element fitted and then made predictions about the properties of the elements that should occupy these gaps.

(a) Predict whether astatine (atomic number 85) is likely to be a solid, a liquid or a gas at room temperature.

(b) Predict a chemical property of caesium (atomic number 55).

25. Certain chemicals are added to petrol to prevent "pinking" in car engines.

Pinking means that the petrol-air mixture explodes too soon.

It is found that iodine compounds are more effective in preventing pinking than bromine or chlorine compounds.

Compounds of selenium (atomic number 34) and tellurium (atomic number 52) are both more effective than iodine compounds, with tellurium compounds better than selenium compounds.

Use this information to explain why the lead compound, tetraethyl lead, is added to some petrols to prevent "pinking".

26. The halogens are the elements in Group 7 of the Periodic Table. Their compounds are known as halides.

Stuart was investigating the reactions between dilute solutions of certain halogens and halides. He added bromine to an iodide and found that iodine was displaced. When he added bromine to a chloride, no reaction took place.

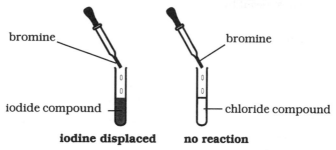

He carried out more experiments and the results of his investigations are summarised in the following table.

		Halide		
		iodide	bromide	chloride
Halogen	chlorine	√	√	×
	bromine	√	×	×
	iodine	×	×	×

√ = displacement reaction   × = no reaction

(a) Use this information to write a general statement about displacement reactions between halogens and halides.

(b) Predict what would happen if chlorine was added to a fluoride.

27. Refer to page 5 of the data booklet.

(a) For each of the compounds shown, decide whether or not 5 g will dissolve in 1 litre of water at room temperature.

Use one of the following letters for your answer.

A   All the solid will dissolve.

B   Only some of the solid will dissolve.

C   Not enough information is given to decide.

(i) calcium oxide   (ii) lead(II) iodide   (iii) potassium chloride

(b) The following compounds are not shown in the data booklet. For each compound predict which letter, vs, s or i, would be used in the table to indicate its solubility.

(i) rubidium chloride   (ii) radium sulphate

Topic 4 How Atoms Combine

General Level

1. Explain what is meant by
   (a) a molecule,
   (b) a covalent bond,
   (c) a chemical formula.

2. Which of the following compounds are made up of molecules?

(a)	sodium chloride	(b)	hydrogen chloride
(c)	carbon sulphide	(d)	aluminium nitrate
(e)	iron oxide	(f)	phosphorus oxide
(g)	copper sulphate	(h)	CH_3Cl
(i)	MgO	(j)	NO_2
(k)	$FeCl_2$	(l)	C_2H_5OH
(m)	Na_2CO_3	(n)	$C_6H_{12}O_6$

3. (a) Explain what is meant by a diatomic molecule.
   (b) Which of the following elements exist as diatomic molecules?

A	calcium	B	carbon	C	nitrogen
D	aluminium	E	hydrogen	F	neon
G	chlorine	H	sulphur	I	magnesium
J	oxygen	K	fluorine	L	argon

Credit Level

4. Draw diagrams to show how the outer electrons form covalent bonds in each of the following molecules.

   (a) hydrogen   (b) oxygen

   (c) nitrogen   (d) carbon fluoride

   (e) hydrogen chloride   (f) hydrogen oxide

   (g) phosphorus chloride   (h) carbon dioxide

5. The atoms in a hydrogen molecule are held together by a covalent bond.

   A covalent bond is a shared pair of electrons.

   Explain how this holds the atoms together.

   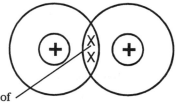

   shared pair of electrons

6. (a) Make a drawing to show the shape of each of the following molecules.

   (i) N_2 (ii) CCl_4 (iii) NH_3 (iv) H_2O

   (b) Name the molecule in (a) which is

   (i) linear,   (ii) flat.

   (c) What name is given to the shape of a CCl_4 molecule?

7.

Gas	Relative atomic mass	Density (relative to hydrogen)
hydrogen	1	1
helium	4	2
nitrogen	14	14
oxygen	16	16
neon	20	10
chlorine	35.5	35.5
argon	40	20

   (a) Some of the gases in the table are made up of diatomic molecules.

   What general statement can be made about the relationship between the relative atomic mass and density (relative to hydrogen) for the diatomic molecules?

   (b) If the relative atomic mass of xenon is 131, predict its density (relative to hydrogen).

Topic 5   Fuels

General Level

1. A substance **X** was heated as shown.

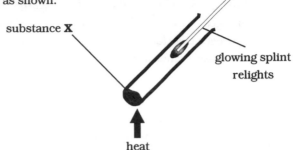

    substance **X**

    glowing splint
    relights

    heat

    (a)   Which gas is produced when **X** is heated?
    (b)   From this experiment, what can be learned about **X**?

2. Petrol is an important <u>fuel</u>. The <u>combustion</u> of petrol is an example of an
    <u>exothermic</u> reaction.
    Explain what is meant by each of the terms underlined.

3. Many important fuels are obtained from crude oil.
    (a)   Describe how crude oil is formed.
    (b)   Explain why crude oil can be described as
          (i)   a fossil fuel,   (ii)   a finite resource.
    (c)   Give **two** examples of pollution problems associated with oil.
    (d)   Name **two** other fossil fuels.

4. You are given three unlabelled cylinders of gas.
    Each cylinder contains one of the following gases.

                oxygen,   nitrogen,   carbon dioxide

    Describe how to find out which gas is contained in each cylinder.

5. Crude oil is a mixture of chemical compounds. Before
    the compounds can be used, the crude oil must be
    separated into fractions, by fractional distillation.
    (a)   Name the kind of chemical
          compounds found in crude oil.
    (b)   Explain what is meant by
          (i)   fractional distillation,
          (ii)   a fraction.   crude oil →
    (c)   Give a use for each of the following products
          obtained from oil.
          (i)   petrol   (ii)   diesel   (iii) gas
          (iv)   kerosine   (v)   bitumen

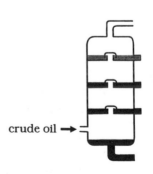

6. (a) Explain what is meant by
    (i) a flammable substance,
    (ii) a viscous substance.
   (b) Consider the following substances obtained from oil:

   petrol, diesel, gas, kerosine, bitumen

   Name the fraction which is
    (i) most flammable,
    (ii) most viscous.

7. A gas is burned and a product collected as shown in the diagram.

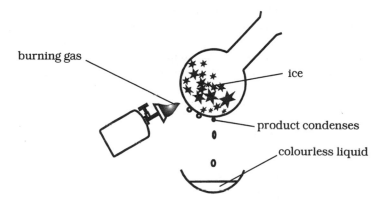

burning gas

ice

product condenses

colourless liquid

Describe how to find out whether or not the colourless liquid is water.

8. (a) Name the **two** gases which are the main components of air.
   (b) What is the approximate percentage of each in air?
   (c) Explain why these gases can combine inside a car engine.

9. Powdered limestone (calcium carbonate) is used to remove sulphur dioxide from the gases given off in a coal fired power station.
   Limestone is insoluble in water. A soluble carbonate would be more efficient.
   (a) Why should sulphur dioxide be removed?
   (b) Suggest why limestone is used rather than a soluble carbonate.

10. In a paraffin burner, heat is produced when the paraffin burns.
    (a) What term is used to describe a reaction which produces heat?
    (b) Which gas is used up when paraffin burns?
    (c) What are the **two** products when paraffin burns in plenty of air?
    (d) Explain why it is dangerous to burn paraffin in a very poorly ventilated room.

11. The burning of petrol can cause pollution of the air.
    (a) Name the poisonous gas which can be formed by the incomplete combustion of petrol.
    (b) Name the poisonous gas which can be formed from sulphur compounds when petrol is burned.
    (c) Name an "additive" to petrol which causes pollution.
    (d) Explain why air pollution is more of a problem in industrial areas.
    (e) State **two** ways of reducing air pollution from the burning of the hydrocarbons in petrol.

12. British motorists throw away about 30 million old rubber tyres every year. Two ways of recycling old tyres are being tried.
    (1) Burn them in power stations where sulphur dioxide formed can be taken out.
    (2) Break up the long chain molecules by heating the tyres to a high temperature in the absence of air. This produces a mixture of hydrocarbon molecules.
    (a) Name **three** elements present in the rubber.
    (b) Name the process which could be used to separate the hydrocarbon molecules in the mixture into useful groups.

13. Fires in coal mines can be caused by coal dust.
    (a) Describe how coal is formed.
    (b) Which element in air is needed for the coal dust to burn?
    (c) Why is coal dust likely to cause explosions?
    (d) In a limited supply of air, coal fires can produce a poisonous gas. Name this gas.

14. Coal is a source of other chemicals.

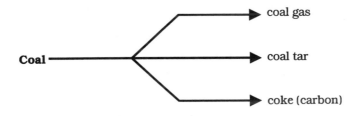

    (a) Coal gas is a mixture of hydrogen and carbon monoxide.
        These gases can be combined to form methanal
            hydrogen + carbon monoxide   →   methanal
        Name **all** the elements present in methanal.
    (b) Coal tar contains hydrocarbons.
        Explain what is meant by a hydrocarbon.
    (c) Give a use for coke (carbon).

15.

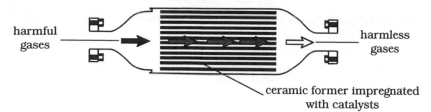

ceramic former impregnated
with catalysts

Catalytic converters in cars can help to reduce pollution. Harmful gases react as they pass over the catalyst.

Here is a typical converter reaction.

$$CO\ (g)\ +\ NO\ (g)\ \xrightarrow{\text{catalyst}}\ CO_2\ (g)\ +\ N_2\ (g)$$

(a) Why does burning petrol in a car engine produce carbon monoxide as well as carbon dioxide?

(b) Suggest why the catalyst is spread over a large surface area.

(c) Give another way by which pollution from a car engine can be reduced.

16. A pupil wanted to investigate whether a paint absorbs air when it dries. The apparatus shown below was used.

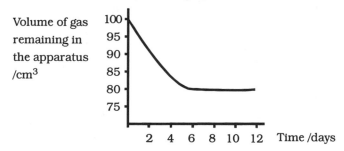

syringe   syringe

glass slides covered in
wet gloss paint

At the start of the experiment, the total volume of air inside the apparatus was 100 cm³. Every day the air in the apparatus was passed back and forth over the painted glass slides. The remaining volume of gas in the apparatus was measured. The results are shown in the graph below.

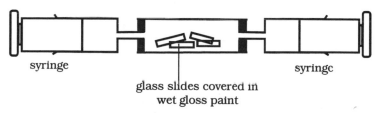

(a) (i) Name the gas which is most likely to have reacted with the paint.

   (ii) Explain your answer.

(b) This paint is normally dry to the touch after 1 day.

   In this experiment, the paint was still sticky after 1 day.

   Suggest a reason for this difference.

17. The small carbon dioxide cylinders which are used to make fizzy drinks can also provide a supply of the gas for experiments.

Carbon dioxide is denser than air.

(a) Identify the most suitable arrangement for collecting a sample of carbon dioxide.

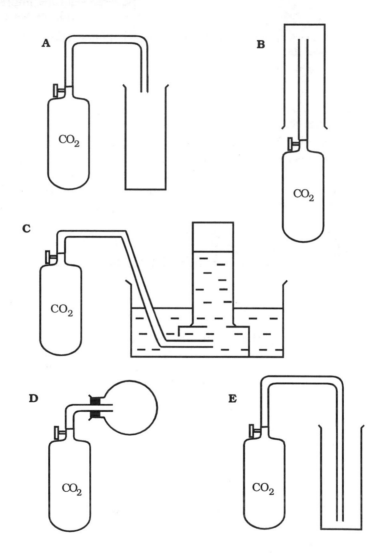

(b) Explain why each of the other arrangements is less suitable than the arrangement chosen in part (a).

18. Crude oil contains a mixture of chemicals. The table compares the composition of a sample of crude oil from the North Sea with one from an oil field in the Middle East.

Chemicals	% of chemicals in two samples of oil	
	North Sea crude	Middle East crude
gases and gasoline	7	6
petroleum spirit	20	14
kerosene and diesel	30	25
residue chemicals	43	55

(a) Copy and label the pie chart below. It shows the composition of **one** of the above samples of crude oil.

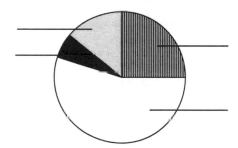

(b) Which sample of crude oil has the composition shown in the pie chart?

(c) Use the information in the table to suggest **one** reason why North Sea crude oil might be more useful than Middle East crude oil for modern day needs.

(d) Name the process used to separate the different chemicals in crude oil.

19. The approximate composition of air is nitrogen 80% and oxygen 20%.

(a) Draw a pie chart to show the proportion of nitrogen to oxygen in the air. Label the gases.

(b) Some bags of potato crisps are filled with pure nitrogen gas instead of air. Suggest why this is done.

20. Sulphur dioxide is one of the causes of acid rain. The bar graph shows the amount of sulphur dioxide released during four years from burning coal in the UK.

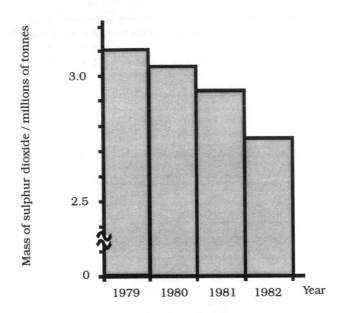

(a) Describe the trend shown by the bar graph.

(b) Suggest **one** reason for this trend.

(c) Sulphur dioxide can also be produced from burning petrol.

    (i) Name **two** other pollutants which can be found in car exhaust fumes.

    (ii) Describe how each gas is produced.

21. The table shows the percentage of energy consumed in the world from various sources in 1987.

Nuclear	Hydro electric	Gas	Coal	Oil
5	7	19	29	40

(a) Draw a **bar graph** to show this information.

(b) What percentage of World energy consumption in 1987 came from fossil fuels?

Credit Level

22. Copy and complete the following.

    The combustion of methane is an _____ reaction, that is, _____ is released. During this reaction, energy is required to _____ bonds in the _____ molecules. Energy is then _____ as the bonds are formed in the product molecules. In this type of reaction, more energy is released in the bond-_____ step then is required in the bond-_____ step.

23. Consider the following substances obtained from fractions of crude oil:

    petrol, diesel, kerosine, gas, bitumen

    (a) Name the substance which contains molecules with carbon atoms in the following ranges.

    (i) C1 to C4   (ii) C4 to C12   (iii) C9 to C16

    (iv) C15 to C25   (v) more than C70

    (b) (i) Which has the higher boiling point, petrol or bitumen?

    (ii) Explain your answer.

    (c) (i) Which is more flammable, gas or kerosine?

    (ii) Explain your answer.

    (d) (i) Which is more viscous, petrol or diesel?

    (ii) Explain your answer.

24. A liquid **X** is made of only two elements. It burns to produce two products. One is a colourless liquid which melts at 0°C and boils at 100°C; the second turns lime water milky.

    (a) Name the two products.

    (b) (i) Name the two elements contained in liquid **X**.

    (ii) Explain your answer.

25. Air pollution from the burning of petrol in a car engine can be reduced by
    (1) using special exhaust systems,
    (2) improving the efficiency of combustion.

    (a) Describe how an exhaust system can be altered so that pollutant gases react to form harmless gases.

    (b) Describe how the efficiency of combustion can be improved.

26. When sodium hydrogen carbonate (bicarbonate of soda) is heated strongly, it decomposes.

    You have to carry out an experiment to prove that carbon dioxide and water vapour are produced.

    Draw a labelled diagram of the apparatus which you would use to show how the experiment could be carried out.

27. The following graphs show how the concentrations of some gases in car exhaust fumes vary with the air to fuel ratio of the mixture which is burned in the engine.

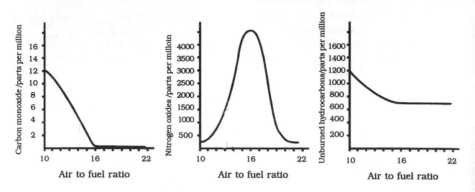

(a) Suggest why the carbon monoxide concentration approaches zero as the air to fuel ratio increases.

(b) Many car engines use an air to fuel ratio of 13.

Which of the gases has the highest concentration in car exhaust fumes using this air to fuel ratio?

(c) Use the information from the graphs to give the advantage of increasing the air to fuel ratio from 18 to 20.

28. Natural gas is readily available in the laboratory.

To burn the gas, it is bubbled through water to monitor the flow rate, then passed through lumps of calcium chloride to dry it.

Copy and complete a labelled diagram to show the arrangement you would use to do this.

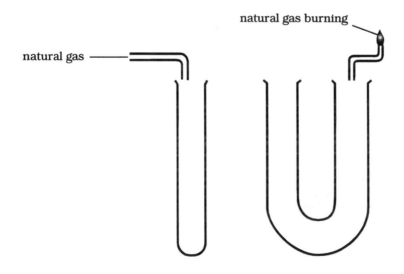

natural gas burning

natural gas

29. A group of pupils undertook a project on acid rain. They designed the following apparatus to compare the amount of sulphur dioxide released from samples of different solid fuels. The sulphur dioxide changed the orange sodium dichromate solution to a green colour.

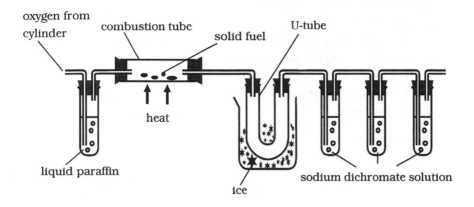

(a) Droplets of water were always detected in the U-tube.

What does this indicate about solid fuels?

(b) Suggest a reason why the pupils designed the apparatus with **more than one** test tube of sodium dichromate solution.

(c) Suggest a reason why the oxygen is bubbled through liquid paraffin before entering the combustion tube.

Topic 6   Structure and Reactions of
General Level   Hydrocarbons

1. Name **three** alkanes and state a use for each.

2. (a) Explain what is meant by
    (i)   a saturated hydrocarbon,   (ii)   an unsaturated hydrocarbon.
    (b) Consider this list of hydrocarbons:
        butane,   ethene,   octane,   methane,   butene
        Name the hydrocarbons which are
        (i)   saturated,   (ii)   unsaturated.

3. Name each of the following molecules.
    (a)   (b)
    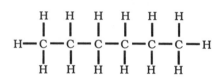

    (c) $CH_3CH_2CH_2CH_2CH_3$ (d) $CH_3CH=CHCH_3$

4. For each of the following molecules
    (a)   propene
    (b)   methane
    (c)   ethene
    (d)   butane
    (i)   draw the **full** structural formula,
    (ii) draw the **shortened** structural formula.

5. State the molecular formula for each of the following straight chain
    hydrocarbons.
    (a)   octane
    (b)   hexene
    (c)   the saturated hydrocarbon with 12 carbon atoms per molecule
    (d)   the unsaturated hydrocarbon with 10 carbon atoms per molecule

6. C_2H_4 + Br_2 →   **X**

    (a)   Draw the full structural formula for substance **X**?
    (b)   What name is given to this type of chemical reaction?
    (c)   Name the product of the reaction of C_2H_4 with H_2.

7. An example of cracking is shown in the equation below.

$$C_8H_{18} \rightarrow C_6H_{14} + \underline{}$$
$$\text{A} \qquad\qquad \text{B} \qquad\qquad \text{C}$$

(a) Explain what is meant by cracking.

(b) Draw a labelled diagram to show how the cracking of hydrocarbon **A** can be carried out in the laboratory. Show how the gas **C** can be collected.

(c) Name a catalyst that can be used to speed up the reaction.

(d) Name the hydrocarbons **A** and **B**.

(e) What is the formula and the name of **C**?

(f) Describe an experiment which can be used to distinguish between **A** and **C**.

(g) Explain why cracking is one of the important processes carried out in an oil refinery.

8. $$C_3H_6 + Br_2 \rightarrow C_3H_6Br_2$$

(a) Is the hydrocarbon C_3H_6 saturated or unsaturated?

(b) What name is given to the above type of chemical reaction?

(c) Draw the full structural formula for the product of the reaction.

9. (a) A liquid hydrocarbon is burned in a plentiful supply of air. Which gases are produced?

(b) The hydrocarbon has no immediate effect of bromine water. What does this indicate?

(c) The hydrocarbon is used in the following apparatus.

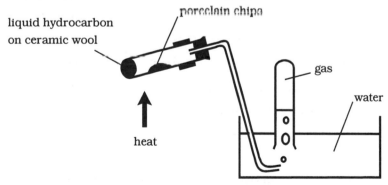

(i) The gas collected rapidly decolourises bromine water. Why is this?

(ii) Name the chemical reaction occurring in the heated tube.

(iii) As soon as heating is stopped what precaution must be taken? Explain why this is necessary.

10. One of the first anaesthetics to be used was chloroform ($CHCl_3$).

The table shows the anaesthetic effect of methane and some chlorine compounds (like chloroform) which are based on methane.

Compound	Anaesthetic effect
CH_4	none
CH_3Cl	weak
CH_2Cl_2	moderate
$CHCl_3$	strong

(a) Using the information in the table, what general statement can be made about the compounds and their anaesthetic effect?

(b) Draw the full structural formula for $CHCl_3$.

11. White spirit (turpentine substitute) is used as paint thinner. Both saturated and unsaturated hydrocarbons are present in white spirit.

Describe how you would test white spirit to show that it contains unsaturated hydrocarbons.

12. The table gives information about the catalysts which are used for some reactions.

Reaction	Catalyst
$CH_4 + H_2O \rightarrow CO + 3H_2$	nickel
$C_2H_5OH \rightarrow C_2H_4 + H_2O$	silicon dioxide
burning of hydrocarbons in car exhausts	platinum
$C_2H_4 + H_2 \rightarrow C_2H_6$	nickel
cracking of hydrocarbons	silicon dioxide
$2H_2 + O_2 \rightarrow 2H_2O$	platinum

Use the information in the table to name a catalyst which would be suitable for each of the following reactions.

(a) $2C_8H_{18} + 25O_2 \rightarrow 16CO_2 + 18H_2O$

(b) $C_6H_6 + 3H_2 \rightarrow C_6H_{12}$

(c) $C_6H_{14} \rightarrow CH_4 + C_5H_{10}$

13. The boiling points of some alkanes are given in the table below.

Alkane	Boiling point / K
methane	109
ethane	185
propane	231
butane	273
hexane	342

(a) Draw a **bar graph** to show this information.

(b) Use your graph to estimate the boiling point of pentane.

(c) You now have information about six alkanes, including pentane.
Name the alkanes which are liquids at 250 K.

14. Here is some information about a series of compounds called alkynes.

Number of carbon atoms	Formula mass
2	26
3	40
4	54
5	68

(a) Draw a **bar graph** to show this information.

(b) Using either the information in the table or your bar graph, state the
formula mass of the alkyne with 6 carbon atoms.

(c) From the information in the table, state the formula for the alkyne with
2 carbon atoms.

15. Naphtha can be cracked to give a number of useful products. A typical result is
shown in the table.

Product	Methane	Ethene	Propene	Petrol	Other products
% by mass	15	25	16	28	15

(a) Draw a **bar graph** to show this result.

(b) Name the family of hydrocarbons to which ethene and propene belong.

16. Some doctors recommend thar we eat unsaturated vegetable oils rather than saturated oils. There is evidence to suggest that this reduces the risk of heart disease.

Each oil is given an "iodine value". This is the volume of iodine solution which is decolourised by 10 cm^3 of oil.

You are given the following apparatus.

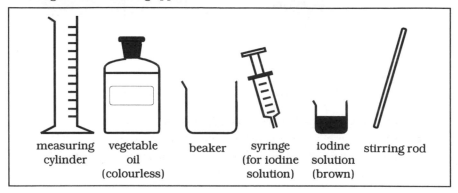

| measuring cylinder | vegetable oil (colourless) | beaker | syringe (for iodine solution) | iodine solution (brown) | stirring rod |

Suggest how you would use this apparatus to find the iodine value of the oil.

17. There are many chemical compounds containing the elements carbon, hydrogen and oxygen. The extended structural formulae for three such compounds are shown.

A

```
    H   H   H
    |   |   |
H — C — C — C — O — H
    |   |   |
    H   H   H
```

B

```
    H   H   O
    |   |   ||
H — C — C — C — H
    |   |
    H   H
```

C

```
    H   O   H
    |   ||  |
H — C — C — C — H
    |       |
    H       H
```

A class carried out experiments with each of the compounds. One pupil's results are shown.

Compound	Reaction with sodium	Effect on acidified potassium permanganate	Flammable or not flammable
A	gas produced	goes colourless	flammable
B	no reaction	goes colourless	flammable
C	no reaction	none	flammable

(a) From the results, what general statement can be made about all three compounds?

(b) From the results, describe how to distinguish **A** from **B**.

(c) Predict what will happen when acidified potassium permanganate is added to a compound with the structure shown.

```
    H   O   H   H
    |   ||  |   |
H — C — C — C — C — H
    |       |   |
    H       H   H
```

18. OCTANE NUMBERS

A way of grading types of petrol is to use "octane numbers". The higher the octane number, the more efficiently the petrol burns.

Some hydrocarbons were tested in an experimental car engine and were found to have octane numbers as shown.

Hydrocarbon	Octane Number
| ```
H   H   H   H   H   H   H
|   |   |   |   |   |   |
H-C — C — C — C — C — C — C-H
|   |   |   |   |   |   |
H   H   H   H   H   H   H
``` | 0 |
| ```
H   H   H   H   H   H   H
|   |   |   |   |   |   |
H-C — C — C — C — C — C — C-H
|   |   |   |   |   |   |
H       H   H   H   H   H
    H-C-H
      |
      H
``` | 22 |
| ```
H   H   H   H   H   H
|   |   |   |   |   |
H-C — C — C — C — C — C-H
|   |   |   |   |   |
H   H   H   H   H   H
``` | 25 |
| ```
H   H   H   H   H
|   |   |   |   |
H-C — C — C — C — C — H
|   |   |   |   |
H       H       H
    H-C-H   H-C-H
      |       |
      H       H
``` | 65 |
| ```
H   H   H   H   H   H
|   |   |   |   |   |
H-C — C — C — C — C — C — H
|   |   |   |   |
H   H-C-H   H   H   H   H
      |
      H
``` | 73 |
| ```
                H
                |
            H-C-H
H   H   H   |   H
|   |   |   |   |
H-C — C — C — C — C — H
|   |   |   |   |
H   H-C-H   H   H-C-H   H
      |           |
      H           H
``` | 100 |

(a) Name the hydrocarbon with an octane number of 25.

(b) State **two** features of the molecular structure which give a high octane number.

19. Gasoline and gas oil are two of the fractions which can be obtained from crude oil. Gas oil can be cracked to give more gasoline.

 (a) State **two** ways in which the molecules produced by cracking can be different from the molecules in gas oil.

 (b) The chart shows the fractions supplied by distilling crude oil and the demand for these fractions.

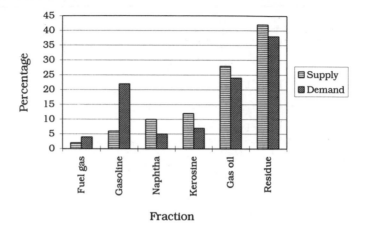

Explain why gas oil is cracked to produce gasoline.

Credit Level

20. The molecular formulae for some alkane molecules are shown.

   C_2H_6 　　　　 CH_4 　　　　 $C_{10}H_{22}$ 　　　　 C_4H_{10}

   (a) Arrange the molecules in order of increasing boiling point (putting the molecule with the lowest boiling point first).

   (b) Explain why the boiling points for alkanes change in this way.

21. (a) Explain what is meant by a homologous series.

   (b) In each of the following lists of hydrocarbons identify the one which is in a different homologous series from the others.

   　(i) ethane, butene, methane, octane

   　(ii) C_3H_8, 　 CH_4, 　 C_7H_{14}, 　 $C_{12}H_{26}$

   　(iii) C_2H_4, 　 C_6H_{12}, 　 CH_4, 　 C_4H_8

22. (a) Are the cycloalkanes saturated or unsaturated?

   (b) What is the formula for the cycloalkane with 12 carbon atoms per molecule?

   (c) Draw the full structural formula for each of the following molecules.

   　(i) cyclobutane 　　　　　　 (ii) cyclohexane

23. Three different hydrocarbons were treated with bromine solution. Each of the hydrocarbons contained six carbon atoms. The results are shown.

Formula	Hydrocarbon	Effect on bromine
C_6H_{12}	A	decolourises quickly
C_6H_{14}	B	no immediate change
C_6H_{12}	C	no immediate change

   Give the names and draw possible structures for **A**, **B** and **C**.

24. Terpenes are important in the perfume industry. One example is terpinolene, an unsaturated hydrocarbon with the molecular formula $C_{10}H_{16}$. The structural formula is shown.

   (a) What is meant by an unsaturated hydrocarbon?

   (b) Write the molecular formula for the product of the complete reaction of terpinolene with bromine.

25. (a) Explain what is meant by isomers.

   (b) Illustrate your answer by drawing isomers of butane.

26. State whether each of the following pairs of molecules are
A isomers **B** **not** isomers.

(i)

```
    H   H   H                      H   H
    |   |   |                      |   |
H—C — C — C—H              H—C — C—H
    |   |   |                      |   |
    H   H   H                      H   H
```

(ii)

```
    H   H                          H   H
    |   |                          |   |
    C ═ C                      H—C — C—H
    |   |                          |   |
    H   H                          H   H
```

(iii)

```
    H   H   H   H                  H   H H
    |   |   |   |                  |   |/
H—C — C — C — C—H          H—C — C   H
    |   |   |   |                  |   |   |
    H   H   H   H                  H   C — C—H
                                      /|   |
                                   H H   H
```

(iv)

```
    H   H   H   H                  H   H   H
    |   |   |   |                  |   |   |
H—C — C — C — C—H          H—C — C — C—H
    |   |   |   |                  |   |   |
    H   |   H   H                  H   |   H
        |                              |
    H —C—H                        H —C—H
        |                              |
        H                         H —C—H
                                      |
                                      H
```

(v)

```
    H   H H                        H
    |   |/                         |
H—C — C   H H                  H—C—H
    |   |   |   |                  |
    H   C — C — C—H            H—C—H
       /|   |   |                  |
      H H   H   H                  H   H
                                   |   |   |
                              H —C — C — C—H
                                   |   |   |
                                   H   H   H
```

(vi)

```
    H   H                          H   H
    |   |                           \ /
H—C — C—H                        C   H   H
    |   |                          ‖   |   |
H—C — C—H                        C — C — C—H
    |   |                          |   |   |
    H   H                          H   H   H
```

(vii)

```
        H                              H
        |                              |
      H-C-H                          H-C-H
      H   H                       H   H
      |   |                       |   |
    H-C - C - C-H              H-C - C - C-H
      H       H                   H   H
        H-C-H                         H-C-H
          |                             |
          H                             H
```

(viii)

```
      H   H                      H   H   H
       \ /                       |   |   |
        C                      H-C - C - C-H
       / \                       |   |   |
    H-C - C-H                    H   H   H
      |   |
      H   H
```

(ix)

```
    H   H                       H   H
     \ /                         |   |       H
      C      H   H             H-C - C - C
      ||     |   |               |   |   ||
      C - C - C-H                H   H   C
     /    |   |                         / \
    H     H   H                        H   H
```

(x)

```
    H   H                        H               H
     \ /                         |               |
      C     H   H              H-C - C = C - C-H
      ||    |   |                |   |   |   |
      C - C - C-H                H   H   H   H
     /    |   |
    H     H   H
```

(xi)

```
      H   H                      H   Cl
      |   |                      |   |
   Cl-C - C-Cl                 H-C - C-H
      |   |                      |   |
      H   H                      Cl  H
```

(xii)

```
     Cl  Cl                     Cl   H
     |   |                      |    |
   H-C - C-H                  Cl-C - C-H
     |   |                      |    |
     H   H                      H    H
```

Structure and Reactions of Hydrocarbons   43

27. Draw the full structural formulae for each of the following.
   (a) **three** isomers of pentane
   (b) **five** isomers of C_4H_8
   (c) **three** isomers of cyclobutane

28. The cracking of paraffin can be carried out in the laboratory using strong heat. A mixture of saturated and unsaturated products is obtained.
   (a) What effect would a suitable catalyst have on the amount of heat needed to crack paraffin?
   (b) Explain why cracking produces a mixture of saturated and unsaturated products.

29. Pyrolysis can be used to convert waste plastics into useful products.
   In this process, the plastics are decomposed by heating in the absence of air.

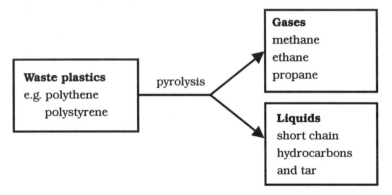

   (a) Methane, ethane and propane are the first three members of the alkane series.

      What general name is give to a series of compounds like the alkanes?
   (b) Name **two** elements found in plastics.
   (c) Suggest why air must be absent during pyrolysis.
   (d) Copy and complete the diagram to show how a sample of the products of pyrolysis can be collected with the liquids separate from the gases.

      Normal laboratory apparatus should be used and clearly labelled.

      No gas should be allowed to escape.

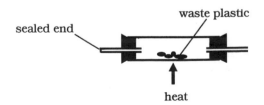

30. Some examples of alkanols are shown.

$$H-\underset{\underset{H}{|}}{\overset{\overset{H}{|}}{C}}-\underset{\underset{H}{|}}{\overset{\overset{H}{|}}{C}}-\underset{\underset{H}{|}}{\overset{\overset{H}{|}}{C}}-OH$$ propan-1-ol

$$H-\underset{\underset{H}{|}}{\overset{\overset{H}{|}}{C}}-\underset{\underset{OH}{|}}{\overset{\overset{H}{|}}{C}}-\underset{\underset{H}{|}}{\overset{\overset{H}{|}}{C}}-H$$ propan-2-ol

$$H-\underset{\underset{H}{|}}{\overset{\overset{H}{|}}{C}}-\underset{\underset{H}{|}}{\overset{\overset{H}{|}}{C}}-\underset{\underset{H}{|}}{\overset{\overset{H}{|}}{C}}-\underset{\underset{H}{|}}{\overset{\overset{H}{|}}{C}}-\underset{\underset{H}{|}}{\overset{\overset{H}{|}}{C}}-OH$$ pentan-1-ol

$$H-\underset{\underset{H}{|}}{\overset{\overset{H}{|}}{C}}-\underset{\underset{H}{|}}{\overset{\overset{H}{|}}{C}}-\underset{\underset{H}{|}}{\overset{\overset{H}{|}}{C}}-\underset{\underset{H}{|}}{\overset{\overset{H}{|}}{C}}-\underset{\underset{H}{|}}{\overset{\overset{H}{|}}{C}}-H$$ pentan-2-ol

$$H-\underset{\underset{H}{|}}{\overset{\overset{H}{|}}{C}}-\underset{\underset{H}{|}}{\overset{\overset{H}{|}}{C}}-\underset{\underset{OH}{|}}{\overset{\overset{H}{|}}{C}}-\underset{\underset{H}{|}}{\overset{\overset{H}{|}}{C}}-\underset{\underset{H}{|}}{\overset{\overset{H}{|}}{C}}-H$$ pentan-3-ol

(a) Give a general formula for these alkanols.

(b) Name the following alkanol.

$$H-\underset{\underset{H}{|}}{\overset{\overset{H}{|}}{C}}-\underset{\underset{H}{|}}{\overset{\overset{H}{|}}{C}}-\underset{\underset{H}{|}}{\overset{\overset{H}{|}}{C}}-\underset{\underset{H}{|}}{\overset{\overset{H}{|}}{C}}-\underset{\underset{OH}{|}}{\overset{\overset{H}{|}}{C}}-\underset{\underset{H}{|}}{\overset{\overset{H}{|}}{C}}-H$$

(c) Water and a straight chain hydrocarbon are the only products formed by the dehydration of propan-1-ol.

Name this hydrocarbon.

31. The full structural formulae below represent two members of a homologous series of compounds called the cycloalkenes.

cyclobutene   cyclohexene

(a) What is the general formula for the cycloalkene series?

(b) Draw the full structural formula for the cycloalkene with five carbon atoms.

(c) Cyclobutene reacts with bromine solution.

Write the molecular formula for the compound formed.

32. The OXO Process involves the reaction between an alkene and synthesis gas (a mixture of carbon monoxide and hydrogen).

The product is an alcohol (an organic compound with an -OH group) with one carbon atom more than the alkene.

$$CH_3\!-\!CH\!=\!CH_2 \ + \ CO \ + \ 2H_2 \ \rightarrow \ CH_3\!-\!\underset{\underset{CH_2OH}{|}}{CH}\!-\!CH_3$$

an alcohol

(a) Draw the formula for an alkene which would give the following alcohol.

$$CH_3\!-\!\underset{\underset{CH_2OH}{|}}{CH}\!-\!CH_2\!-\!CH_3$$

(b) Draw the formula for the alcohol which would be obtained from ethene.

33. Alkanes can be made by the reaction of sodium with iodoalkanes.

This is called the Wurtz synthesis.

For example, ethane can be made from iodomethane.

(a) Name the alkane which forms when sodium reacts with iodoethane.

(b) Two different iodoalkanes are used to make propane.

Name the two iodoalkanes.

(c) The Wurtz synthesis can also be used to make cycloalkanes.

Draw the full structural formula of the compound which could be used to make cyclobutane.

34. Alkenes can be synthesised by reacting a carbonyl compound with a phosphorus compound.

$$
\begin{array}{c}
R_1 \\
| \\
C=O \\
| \\
R_2
\end{array}
\; + \;
\begin{array}{c}
\quad C_6H_5\; R_3 \\
\quad\;| \quad\; | \\
C_6H_5\!-\!P\!=\!C \\
\quad\;| \quad\; | \\
\quad C_6H_5\; R_4
\end{array}
\;\rightarrow\;
\begin{array}{c}
R_1 \quad R_3 \\
| \qquad | \\
C=C \\
| \qquad | \\
R_2 \quad R_4
\end{array}
\; + \;
\begin{array}{c}
\qquad\quad C_6H_5 \\
\qquad\quad\;| \\
C_6H_5\!-\!P\!=\!O \\
\qquad\quad\;| \\
\qquad\quad C_6H_5
\end{array}
$$

R is a shorthand way of writing a hydrogen atom or an alkane with one hydrogen atom removed,

i.e. $-R$ could be $-H$, $-CH_3$, $-C_2H_5$, $-C_3H_7$, etc.

(a) Draw the structural formula for the alkene formed in the following reaction.

$$
\begin{array}{c}
CH_3 \\
| \\
C=O \\
| \\
CH_3
\end{array}
\; + \;
\begin{array}{c}
\quad C_6H_5\; H \\
\quad\;| \quad\; | \\
C_6H_5\!-\!P\!=\!C \\
\quad\;| \quad\; | \\
\quad C_6H_5\; CH_3
\end{array}
\;\rightarrow
$$

(b) Draw the structural formula for the carbonyl compound that would be used to make ethene.

35. The hydrocarbons present in a mixture can be separated using chromatography. The mixture is vapourised and is then passed through a special column. Different hydrocarbons move through the column at different speeds. The following graph was obtained.

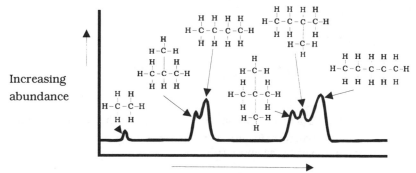

Increasing time to move through the column.

(a) Make **two** general statements linking the structure of the hydrocarbon with the length of time taken to pass through the column.

(b) Copy the graph and show with an arrow, the expected position for propane.

36. The following reaction shows what happens when an alkene reacts with ozone.

```
      H   H   H   H   H                    H   H   H           H   H
      |   |   |   |   |                    |   |   |           |   |
  H — C — C — C = C — C — H  + ozone →  H — C — C — C = O + O = C — C — H
      |   |       |                        |   |   |           |   |
      H   H       H                        H   H   H           H   H
```

(a) Draw the full structural formulae of the products you would expect from the following reaction.

```
      H   H   H   H   H   H
      |   |   |   |   |   |
  H — C — C = C — C — C — C — H  + ozone →
      |           |   |   |
      H           H   H   H
```

(b) Ozonolysis of another molecule gives only **one** product.

Draw the full structural formula of an alkene which would react in this way.

37. Organic chemistry has a number of rules that can help to predict the products of a reaction.

The equation shows what happens when an ionic compound in solution is added to an alkene.

```
      H   H                              H   H
      |   |                              |   |
      C = C   +  H⁺Br⁻(aq)     →     H — C — C — Br
      |   |                              |   |
      H   CH₃                            H   CH₃
```

The positive ion adds on to the double-bonded carbon atom which has the greater number of hydrogen atoms bonded to it.

(a)
```
      H   CH₃
      |   |
      C = C   +  HO⁻Cl⁺(aq)    →     Product
      |   |
      H   CH₃
```

Draw the full structural formula for the product in the above reaction.

(b) Draw the full structural formula for an isomer of butene which could **not** be used to demonstrate the above rule.

38. The first bicycle lamps were not electric. A hydrocarbon gas called acetylene was burned to produce the light.

The acetylene gas was made by adding water to a solid called calcium carbide.

Acetylene gas is insoluble in water.

(a) Name the two products which are formed when acetylene burns in a plentiful supply of oxygen.

(b) Draw a diagram of the apparatus you would use to prepare and collect a gas jar of acetylene in your chemistry laboratory.

Topic 6

39. A pupil carried out a test with a number of organic compounds. The results are shown in the table.

Molecule	Structure	Result of test
A	H–C–C–C–H with H, H on top; H, O(double bond), H on bottom	no reaction
B	H–C–C–H with H on top; H, O(double bond) on bottom	orange precipitate forms
C	H–C–C–C–C–H with H, H, H on top; H, H, O(double bond), H on bottom	no reaction
D	H–C–H with O(double bond) below C	orange precipitate forms

(a) State whether or not an orange precipitate will form with the following molecule.

$$H-C-C-C-C-H$$

with H, H, H on top and H, H, H, O(double bond) on bottom

(b) Molecule **B** (ethanal), molecule **D** (methanal) and pentanal are members of a homologous series called alkanals. The structure of pentanal is:

$$H-C-C-C-C-C-H$$

with H, H, H, H on top and H, H, H, H, O(double bond) on bottom

Give a general formula for the alkanal series of organic compounds.

Topic 7   Properties of Substances

General Level

1. (a) By means of a labelled diagram, show the experimental apparatus which can be used to classify substances into conductors and non-conductors.

   (b) Study the following list of solids

   > nickel, iodine, copper, magnesium, sulphur, phosphorus, sodium, scandium

   Arrange the solids in two columns, headed conductors and non-conductors.

   (c) Study the following list of liquids:

   > petrol, copper sulphate solution, silicon tetrachloride, hexene, liquid oxygen, molten sulphur, sodium chloride solution, mercury, strontium nitrate solution, molten iron

   Arrange the liquids in two columns, headed conductors and non-conductors.

2. Study the following list of substances:

   > glucose, sulphur, sodium bromide, paraffin wax, silicon dioxide, silver, carbon tetrachloride, potassium, nickel chloride

   (a) Name the substances which conduct electricity when solid.

   (b) (i) Name the substances which conduct electricity when in aqueous solution.

   (ii) Explain why the solutions you have chosen do not conduct when solid.

3. The electrical conductivities of substances **A**, **B** and **C** were measured and the results are shown.

Substance	In solid state	Dissolved in water	In molten state
A	0	+	+
B	+	insoluble	+
C	0	0	0

   + conducts well   0 non-conductor

   (a) Which substance could be lead?

   (b) Which substance could be potassium bromide?

   (c) Which substance could be iodine?

4.

	P	Q	R	S
Solubility in water	soluble	insoluble	soluble	soluble
Colour of solution	colourless	-	blue	colourless
Electrical conductivity in solid state	does not conduct	conducts	does not conduct	does not conduct
Electrical conductivity in molten state	does not conduct	conducts	conducts	conducts

Some properties of four substances

        sodium chloride,   copper bromide,   aluminium,   glucose

are given in the table above.

(a)   Use the table to identify the four substances **P**, **Q**, **R**, and **S**.

(b)   State the type of chemical bonding in substances **P**, **R**, and **S**

(c)   Explain why

    (i)   substance **Q** conducts electricity in the solid state,

    (ii) substances **R** and **S** do not conduct when solid but do conduct in the molten state.

5.   (a)   Draw a labelled diagram to show an experiment you would carry out to test whether a substance is ionic or covalent.

     (b)   The table below shows some properties of two chlorides.

Chloride	M.pt. /°C	B.pt. /°C	Solubility in water
XCl	801	1417	soluble
YCl_4	-23	77	insoluble

    (i)   Which of these chlorides would you expect to be covalent and which is likely to be ionic?

    (ii) In which group of the Periodic Table would you expect to find element **X**?

6. A pupil carried out experiments to investigate what happens during the electrolysis of melts.
    (a) Explain what is meant by electrolysis.
    (b) Name the products at the positive and negative electrode in the electrolysis of melts of the following compounds.
         (i) magnesium chloride   (ii) sodium iodide
         (iii) lead bromide   (iv) calcium oxide

7. The compounds **P**, **Q**, **R** and **S** all contain chlorine. Use the information in the table to answer the questions which follow.
    (Assume room temperature to be 25 °C .)

Chloride	P	Q	R	S
Boiling point / °C	1690	62	76	1412
Melting point / °C	1074	-63	-112	708

    (a) Which of these chlorides are liquid at room temperature?
    (b) State which of these has a simple molecular structure.

8. Several groups of pupils carried out the same experiment using the apparatus shown. One group found the results shown in Table 1, while all the other groups found the results shown in Table 2.

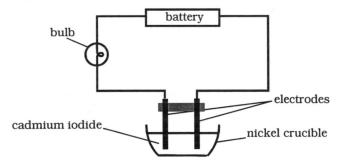

Time	Table 1	Table 2
before heating	bulb not lit	bulb not lit
during heating	bulb lights	bulb lights
when apparatus has cooled	bulb stays lit	bulb goes out

    (a) Explain why most groups obtained the results in Table 2.
    (b) Name the product formed at each electrode.
    (c) Give a possible reason for the faulty results at the end of the experiment in Table 1.

9.

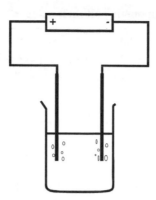

With a battery as a power supply, hydrochloric acid can be electrolysed using carbon electrodes. During the electrolysis, chlorine gas is given off at the positive electrode and hydrogen gas is given off at the negative electrode.

(a) Copy and label the above diagram.

(b) Why is chlorine gas given off at the positive electrode?

(c) Suggest a reason why the electrodes are **not** made of iron.

10. Electricity is used to obtain aluminium from a molten mixture containing bauxite (aluminium oxide).

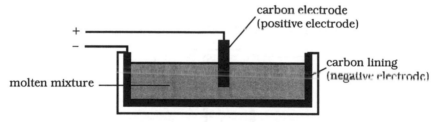

carbon electrode
(positive electrode)

carbon lining
(negative electrode)

+
–

molten mixture

(a) Why does the mixture need to be kept molten?

(b) Explain why aluminium is formed at the negative electrode.

11. Paul connected a low voltage supply to carbon electrodes in a copper chloride solution. He wrote some notes in his jotter.

> Observations
> A gas was given off at the positive electrode.
> The other carbon rod turned brown.

(a) What type of experiment did Paul carry out?

(b) Name the gas given off at the positive electrode.

(c) Explain why the negative electrode "turned brown".

12. Shown below is a list of compounds and their colours.

sodium chloride	white	sodium sulphate	white
sodium selenate	white	copper sulphate	blue
nickel sulphate	green	vanadium sulphate	violet

State the colour of

(a)   copper selenate,   (b)   vanadium chloride,   (c)   nickel chloride.

13. A crystal of copper dichromate was placed on moist filter paper at position **X**. When a high voltage was applied, a blue colour moved towards the negative electrode while an orange colour moved towards the positive electrode.

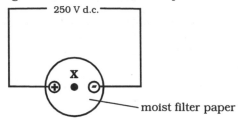

(a)   (i)   What can be learned from this experiment about the colour and charge of the dichromate ion?

(ii)   Explain your answer.

(b)   State any safety precaution which should be observed in this experiment.

14.

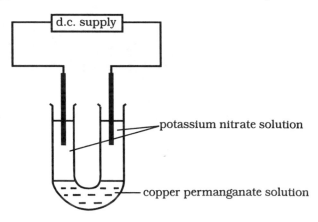

The apparatus shown is used to demonstrate the electrolysis of copper permanganate solution.

(a)   Why is potassium nitrate solution used instead of water?

(b)   Potassium chloride is white while potassium permanganate is purple. What is the colour of the permanganate ion?

(c)   (i)   What will be observed after passing the current in the above apparatus for about 20 minutes?

(ii)   Explain your answer.

15.

wet filter paper — electrodes
-ve — +ve
crystal of green nickel chloride

(a) (i) What will happen when the current is switched on?

    (ii) Explain your answer.

(b) What will happen if the current is reversed?

16. Copy and complete the following table to show the numbers of protons and electrons in each of the following ions.

Ion	Number of protons	Number of electrons
Ca^{2+} Cl^- Al^{3+} O^{2-}		

(b) Look at the information in the table.

Ion	Number of protons	Number of electrons
zinc	30	28
sulphide	16	18
copper	29	28
tin	50	48

Using the information in the table, show how you would represent

    (i) the zinc ion,   (ii) the copper ion,

    (iii) the sulphide ion,   (iv) the tin ion.

17. (a) Explain clearly what happens when

    (i) an atom of chlorine forms a chloride ion,

    (ii) an atom of calcium forms a calcium ion.

(b) What happens during the formation of an ionic bond in calcium chloride?

18. A compound is formed from a Group 1 element and a Group 7 element. Choose two elements and show by means of a diagram what happens to the electrons in the outer energy level (shell) of the atoms involved.

19. Hydrogen chloride is made up of molecules but sodium chloride exists as a lattice.
    (a) Explain what is meant by a lattice.
    (b) Explain why the word "molecule" has no meaning when we are thinking of sodium chloride.

20. An electric current was passed through different solutions. The results are shown in the table.

Solution	Positive electrode product	Negative electrode product
hydrochloric acid	chlorine	hydrogen
potassium chloride	chlorine	hydrogen
sulphuric acid	oxygen	hydrogen
sodium nitrate	oxygen	hydrogen
nitric acid	oxygen	hydrogen
silver nitrate	oxygen	silver

    (a) From the results, suggest a general statement which can be made about acids.
    (b) From the results, predict the products at the positive and negative electrodes, if potassium nitrate is used.
    (c) Explain why potassium chloride conducts electricity when dissolved in water but **not** when solid.

21. Copper(II) sulphate solution is blue. When it is placed in a beam of light, some light is absorbed and some passes through.

    David investigated this effect to see if the amount of light passing through depends on the concentration of the copper(II) sulphate solution.

    He obtained the following results.

Concentration of $CuSO_4$ / moles per litre	0.05	0.2	0.4	0.6	0.8	1.0
Light passing through / %	74.0	29.0	11.0	5.0	3.0	2.0

    (a) Draw a **line graph** to show these results.
    (b) State the relationship between the amount of light passing through and the concentration of the copper(II) sulphate solution.
    (c) Use your graph to estimate the concentration of a copper(II) sulphate solution which allows 50% of the light to pass through.

Credit Level

22. A pupil carried out an experiment to investigate the products of the electrolysis of nickel bromide solution.
    (a) Explain why a d.c. supply is used for this experiment.
    (b) Explain what would be seen at the negative electrode.
    (c) Explain what would be seen at the positive electrode.
    (d) Explain why carbon tetrabromide solution cannot be changed in the same way.

23. A pupil investigated the properties of three compounds. The results are shown in the table.

Substance	Melting point	Electrical conduction
A	high	does not conduct in any state
B	low	does not conduct in any state
C	high	conducts in solution and as melt

Using the information in the table, explain whether the bonding in **A**, **B** and **C** is covalent (small molecule), covalent (network) or ionic.

24. Water in swimming pools can be purified using a chlorinating cell. Sodium chloride solution is electrolysed in the cell to produce chlorine.

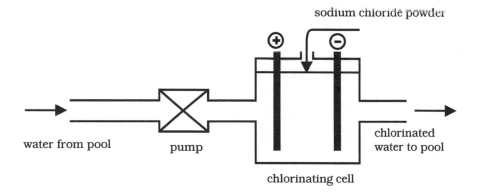

sodium chloride powder

water from pool   pump

chlorinated water to pool

chlorinating cell

    (a) Why can solid sodium chloride **not** be electrolysed?
    (b) (i) At which electrode is chlorine produced?
        (ii) Describe what is happening in the formation of chlorine.

25. Mr Young gave his class three bottles labelled **A**, **B** and **C**.

They contained silver nitrate solution, dilute hydrochloric acid and glucose solution.

He asked the class to use the following apparatus to identify the solutions.

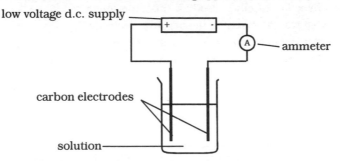

Here are the results for one group of pupils.

Solution	Meter reading	Observations at electrodes
A	no	no reaction
B	yes	grey solid at negative electrode
C	yes	a gas formed at both electrodes

(a) (i) Identify solution **A**.

   (ii) What type of bonding must **A** have?

(b) Identify solution **B**.

(c) Name the gas formed at the positive electrode when solution **C** is used.

26. Explain each of the following.

(a) Sodium oxide is a solid at room temperature.

(b) Carbon dioxide is a gas at room temperature.

(c) Silicon oxide is a solid at room temperature.

27. The average composition of a bottle of drinking water is shown.

Cations	Mass /mg	Anions	Mass /mg
calcium	1	hydrogencarbonate	5
magnesium	1	chloride	25
potassium	3	sulphate	5
sodium	16	nitrate	0

(a) Which cation will give a yellow colour in a flame test?
(You may wish to refer to page 4 of the data booklet to help you.)

(b) What do all these anions have in common.

(c) Suggest a reason for samples of drinking water from various parts of the country having different conductivities.

28. Gillian investigated the ability of different substances to conduct electricity when dissolved in water.

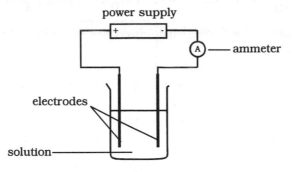

Here are her results.

Substance	Concentration of solution in mol l^{-1}	Current in mA
sodium chloride	0.005	21
sodium chloride	0.002	11
sodium chloride	0.001	7
hydrochloric acid	0.005	62
hydrochloric acid	0.002	27
hydrochloric acid	0.001	20
sodium hydroxide	0.005	32
sodium hydroxide	0.002	15
sodium hydroxide	0.001	11

(a) What name is used to describe a solution which conducts electricity?

(b) Identify **two** variables which she would have kept constant to make sure that her results were fair.

(c) From the results, state the effect of changing concentration on the ability of a substance to conduct electricity when dissolved in water.

(d) Arrange the three substances in order of their ability to conduct electricity when dissolved in water. (Put the best conductor first.)

29. Titanium is used in the making of supersonic aircraft and space vehicles.

To extract titanium, rutile, a titanium ore, is first converted into titanium(IV) chloride. This is then reduced to the metal by heating it with sodium or magnesium in an atmosphere of argon.

(a) Suggest why it is necessary to carry out the reduction of titanium(IV) chloride in an atmosphere of argon.

(b) Titanium(IV) chloride is a liquid at room temperature.
What does this indicate about the type of bonding in titanium(IV) chloride.

30. The following table shows the properties of four substances.

Property	P	Q	R	S
appearance	sparkling solid	silvery liquid	white solid	colourless liquid
solubilty in water	insoluble	insoluble	soluble	soluble
electrical conductivity	does not conduct	conducts when solid or molten	conducts when molten or in solution	does not conduct
melting point /°C	3547	-61	801	-115
boiling point /°C	4827	357	1417	59

For each of **P**, **Q**, **R** and **S**, explain whether the substance is likely to be a metal, an ionic compound or a covalent compound (small molecule or network).

Topic 8   Acids and Alkalis
General Level

1. Weather balloons carrying scientific instruments are sent into the upper
    atmosphere.
    (a) Why can hydrogen and helium be used for filling the balloons?
         You may wish to use the data booklet to help you.
    (b) Suggest why it is dangerous to use hydrogen.

2. (a) What is meant by the pH of a solution?
    (b) Describe how the pH of a solution can be measured.
    (c) What colours do acids turn pH paper?
    (d) What range of pH values can be shown by acids?
    (e) What colours do alkalis turn pH paper?
    (f) What range of pH values can be shown by alkalis?
    (g) What colour do neutral solutions turn pH paper?
    (h) What is the pH of neutral solutions?

3. (a) (i)   Name **three** laboratory acids.
         (ii) Name **three** house-hold solutions which are acidic.
    (b) (i)   Name **three** laboratory alkalis.
         (ii) Name **three** house-hold solutions which are alkalis.

4. The following is a report given by the Wellcare Company to a fish farmer.

    +--+
    | **WELLCARE REPORT** |
    | **Water test** |
    | This showed the water was pH 5. |
    | **Action needed** |
    | The water should be treated to increase the pH |
    +--+

    (a) Describe how you would use Universal indicator or pH paper to measure
         the pH of the water.
    (b) Suggest a cause for the low pH.
    (c) Give the chemical name of a substance which could be used to increase the
         pH of the water.

5. As a homework exercise, pupils were asked to find the pH values of a number of
    substances found in the home.
    One pupil wrote down her results as follows.
    bicarbonate of soda - 9; vinegar - 4; drain cleaner - 14; cola drink - 3; milk - 8;
    indigestion pill - 10; window cleaner - 12; washing-up liquid - 7; lemon juice- 3.
    Present the results of the home exercise in **two** different ways.

6. This graph shows how much lime a gardener needs to add to produce a soil of the desired pH, e.g. if the soil had a pH of 4, but a pH of 7 was required, 1.3 kg of lime would be needed for every 10 m² of soil.

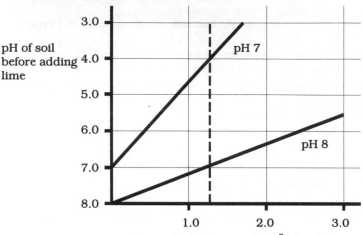

Mass of lime / kg per 10 m² of soil

Find the mass of lime which is needed to increase the pH of soil

(a) from pH 6 to pH 7 in a 10 m² garden,

(b) from pH 7 to pH 8 in a 10 m² garden,

(c) from pH 6 to pH 8 in a 100 m² garden.

7. A gardener tests the pH of the soil in his garden. The soil has a pH of 5.8. The table shows the pH range in which different vegetables will grow successfully.

Vegetable	pH range
broad beans	5.5 - 7.0
carrots	6.0 - 7.5
lettuce	6.5 - 7.5
potatoes	5.5 - 6.5

(a) Which vegetables will the gardener be able to grow successfully in his garden?

(b) Name a substance that the gardener could add to the soil in order to grow all of the vegetables successfully.

8. Explain why crystals of citric acid have no effect on dry pH paper but turn Universal indicator red.

9. Many pollution problems are linked to the release of sulphur dioxide into the air.

(a) What name is given to a solution of sulphur dioxide in rain-water?

(b) Give **three** examples of the damage which can be caused by this solution.

10. Consider the following list:

iron(III) oxide, sodium hydroxide, carbon dioxide,
calcium oxide, nitrogen dioxide, copper(II) oxide

(a) Name **two** substances which dissolve to produce a solution which has a pH below 7.

(b) Name **two** substances which dissolve to produce a solution which has a pH above 7.

11. Two unknown elements **A** and **B** form oxides. The oxide of **A** gives an aqueous solution of pH 5 while the oxide of **B** gives a solution of pH 10.

State what this tells us about

(a) the oxides of **A** and **B**,

(b) the elements **A** and **B**.

12.

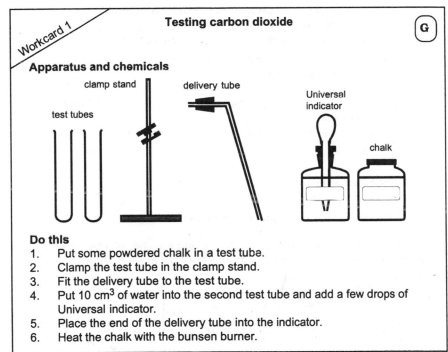

Workcard 1

Testing carbon dioxide

G

Apparatus and chemicals

clamp stand   delivery tube

test tubes

Universal indicator

chalk

Do this
1. Put some powdered chalk in a test tube.
2. Clamp the test tube in the clamp stand.
3. Fit the delivery tube to the test tube.
4. Put 10 cm^3 of water into the second test tube and add a few drops of Universal indicator.
5. Place the end of the delivery tube into the indicator.
6. Heat the chalk with the bunsen burner.

(a) Copy and complete the diagram of the apparatus for the experiment.
Label your diagram to show the chemicals and where you would heat.

(b) What colour would the Universal indicator turn?

13. Using the apparatus shown, a pupil electrolysed three different acid solutions.

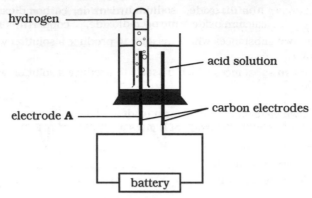

hydrogen

acid solution

carbon electrodes

electrode **A**

battery

It was noted that a gas was given off at electrode **A** in all cases.
The pupil suspects that the gas is hydrogen.

(a) What test would show that the gas collected is hydrogen?

(b) (i) Is **A** the positive or negative electrode?

(ii) Explain your answer.

14. Some battery acid is spilt on the garage floor. Water is added to dilute the solution, before it is wiped up.

(a) Explain why water is added.

(b) What happens to the pH of the solution when water is added?

15. Chlorine reacts with water.

$$Cl_2(g) \quad + \quad H_2O(l) \quad \rightarrow \quad 2H^+(aq) \quad + \quad OCl^-(aq) \quad + \quad Cl^-(aq)$$

What happens to the pH of water when it is chlorinated?

16. Ethanoic acid, found in vinegar, is the second member of a family of acids which all contain carbon. Information about five of the acids is shown.

Acid	Boiling point /°C
A	164
B	141
C	118
D	186
E	102

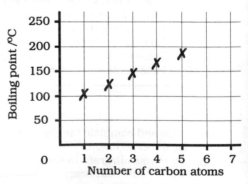

(a) State the number of carbon atoms present in a molecule of **C**.

(b) Estimate the boiling point of the acid with 6 carbon atoms per molecule.

(c) Which ion is present in solutions of all acids?

17. Kirsty eats three meals a day.

The graph shows how much the pH in her mouth varies during the day.

X, Y and **Z** are meal times.

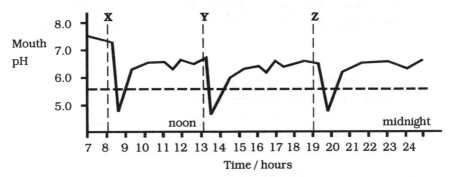

Teeth decay when the pH in the mouth falls below 5.5.

(a) What happens to the pH in the mouth after mealtimes?

(b) Some of Kirsty's friends eat snacks between meals.
Why does this lead to more tooth decay?

(c) Suggest why many toothpastes are alkaline.

18. A bottle has the following label.

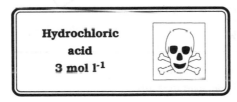

What does the label tell you about the hydrochloric acid?

19. Calculate the formula mass of each of the following substances.

(a) H_2O (b) CH_4

(c) $CaCO_3$ (d) Na_2SO_4

(e) $Mg(NO_3)_2$ (f) nitrogen hydride

(g) carbon dioxide   (h) potassium carbonate

(i) aluminium oxide   (j) ammonium chloride

20. Calculate the mass of one mole of each of the following substances.

(a) C_3H_6 (b) MgO

(c) K_2CO_3 (d) $C_6H_{12}O_6$

(e) $(NH_4)_2SO_4$ (f) magnesium chloride

(g) calcium oxide   (h) potassium hydroxide

(i) magnesium sulphate   (j) sodium nitrate

Credit Level

21. Pure water is added to a solution with a pH of 12.

    (a) Which **two** ions are present in pure water?

    (b) Which contains more hydroxide ions, the solution or the pure water?

    (c) What happens to the concentration of hydroxide ions in the solution as the water is added ?

22. Acid solutions contain $H^+(aq)$ ions; so does pure water.

    (a) Explain why pure water is not an acid.

    (b) When water is added to an acid solution the pH rises.

       (i) Explain why this happens.

       (ii) What is the highest value to which the pH can rise?

       (iii) Explain your answer to (ii).

23. A patient who was undergoing heart surgery had the concentration of carbon dioxide in his blood measured continuously.

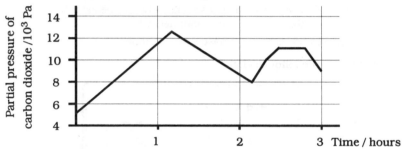

The pH of his blood was also measured.

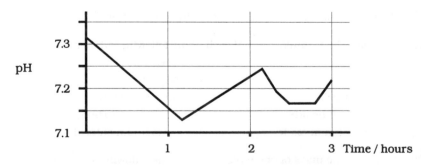

    (a) What happens to the acidity of his blood during the first hour?

    (b) How does the change in concentration of carbon dioxide in his blood affect the pH?

    (c) Carbon dioxide reacts with water.

    $$CO_2(g) \quad + \quad H_2O(l) \quad \rightleftharpoons \quad H^+(aq) \quad + \quad HCO_3^-(aq)$$

    How does the equation explain the effect of an increase in concentration of carbon dioxide on the pH of blood?

                                                               Topic 8

24. Chromium(VI) oxide reacts with water to form chromic acid.

   $CrO_3(s) + H_2O(l) \rightarrow H_2CrO_4(aq)$

   Suggest what is unusual about the reaction between chromium(VI) oxide and water.

25. The following table shows the formula mass of various gases.

Gas	ammonia	argon	carbon monoxide	ethane	oxygen
Formula mass	17	40	28	20	32

   (a) Use your data booklet to find the density of the five gases and draw a **line graph** of density against formula mass.

   (b) A compound of carbon, hydrogen and fluorine has a density of $1.51 \, kg/m^{-3}$.

   (i) Use your line graph to find the formula mass of the gas.

   (ii) Give the formula for this gas.

26. White phosphorus readily catches fire in air.

   The following diagrams show this reaction.

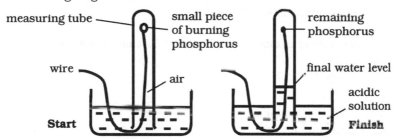

   (a) Why does the reaction produce an acidic solution?

   (b) (i) What would have been the effect on the final water level inside the tube, if a larger piece of phosphorus had been used?

   (ii) Explain your answer.

27. The composition by mass of 9-carat gold is shown in the pie chart.

   A 9 carat-gold ring weighs 7.88 g.

   Calculate the number of moles of gold in the ring.

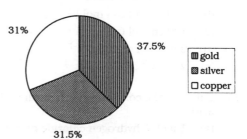

28. Heavy water is made up of molecules in which each of the hydrogen atoms has one neutron in its nucleus.

   Calculate the number of moles of heavy water molecules in 500 g of heavy water.

29. The filling for a tooth is often made of dental amalgam.
The pie chart shows the composition of a typical dental amalgam.

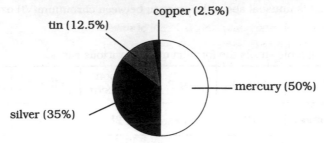

Calculate the number of moles of mercury in 2.0 g of dental amalgam.

30. Calculate the mass of each of the following substances.
    (a) 2 mol of sodium
    (b) 0.1 mol of $CaSO_4$
    (c) 0.25 mol of $MgNO_3$
    (d) 5 mol of sulphur dioxide
    (e) 0.2 mol of magnesium oxide
    (f) 0.5 mol of ammonium carbonate

31. Calculate the number of moles in each of the following substances.
    (a) 36 g of carbon
    (b) 5.6 g of CO
    (c) 4 g of NaOH
    (d) 2.06 g of lithium sulphate
    (e) 8.2 g of calcium nitrate
    (f) 2.9 kg of magnesium hydroxide

32. Calculate the number of moles of potassium hydroxide which must be dissolved
to make each of the following solutions.
    (a) 500 cm^3 of 1 mol l^{-1}
    (b) 200 cm^3 of 0.5 mol l^{-1}
    (c) 100 cm^3 of 0.1 mol l^{-1}
    (d) 2 litres of 0.25 mol l^{-1}
    (e) 250 cm^3 of 2 mol l^{-1}

33. Calculate the concentration of each of the following solutions of hydrochloric
acid.
    (a) 1 mol of hydrogen chloride dissolved to make 100 cm^3 of solution
    (b) 2 mol of hydrogen chloride dissolved to make 1 litre of solution
    (c) 0.1 mol of hydrogen chloride dissolved to make 500 cm^3 of solution
    (d) 0.5 mol of hydrogen chloride dissolved to make 250 cm^3 of solution
    (e) 0.4 mol of hydrogen chloride dissolved to make 200 cm^3 of solution

34. Calculate the volume of each of the following solutions of sodium hydroxide.
    (a) 1 mol l^{-1} solution containing 2 mol of solute
    (b) 0.5 mol l^{-1} solution containing 1 mol of solute
    (c) 2 mol l^{-1} solution containing 0.1 mol of solute
    (d) 0.1 mol l^{-1} solution containing 0.5 mol of solute
    (e) 0.4 mol l^{-1} solution containing 0.1 mol of solute.

35. Calculate the number of grams of substance required to make each of the following solutions.
    (a) 50 cm^3 of NaOH(aq), concentration 2 mol l^{-1}
    (b) 100 cm^3 of KOH(aq), concentration 0.5 mol l^{-1}
    (c) 1 litre of Na_2CO_3(aq), concentration 0.1 mol l^{-1}
    (d) 25 cm^3 of lithium nitrate solution, concentration 0.2 mol l^{-1}
    (e) 250 cm^3 of ammonium sulphate solution, concentration 1 mol l^{-1}
    (f) 200 cm^3 of calcium nitrate solution, concentration 0.25 mol l^{-1}

36. Calculate the concentration of each of the following solutions.
    (a) 5.65 g of NaCl dissolved to make 1 litre of solution
    (b) 2.5 g of $CaCO_3$ dissolved to make 100 cm^3 of solution
    (c) 8 g of NaOH dissolved to make 250 cm^3 of solution
    (d) 2.02 g of potassium nitrate dissolved to make 50 cm^3 of solution
    (e) 4 g of copper(II) sulphate dissolved to make 100 cm^3 of solution
    (f) 1.27 g of iron(II) chloride dissolved to make 2 litres of solution

37. Toners for colouring black and white photographs are made by mixing two solutions. The solutions should be made up using warm water.

Solution 1	Solution 2
Sodium sulphide solution concentration 100 g / l	Sodium hydroxide solution concentration 80 g / l

    (a) Calculate the concentration of the sodium hydroxide solution in mol l^{-1}.
    (b) Different colours are obtained by mixing the two solutions.

	Toner composition	
Colour	Volume of sodium sulphide solution / cm^3	Volume of sodium hydroxide solution / cm^3
cold brown	10	40
brown	20	30
warm brown	30	20

    What mass of sodium sulphide will be required to make 100 cm^3 of toner for a cold brown colour.

Acids and Alkalis   69

Topic 9   Reactions of Acids
General Level

1. (a) Explain what is meant by a neutralisation reaction.
    (b) What happens to the pH of an acid as it is neutralised?
    (c) What happens to the pH of an alkali as it is neutralised?

2. (a) Explain why gardeners add lime to soil which is acidic.
    (b) Explain why Milk of Magnesia is taken to relieve acid indigestion.

3. In certain hard-water areas, scale can build up on the inside of kettles.
    When tested with Universal indicator, the scale shows a pH above 7.
    (a) Explain why vinegar could be used to descale kettles.
    (b) Name the kind of reaction that would occur.
    (c) Name **one** of the products of the reaction.

4. During manned flights in space rockets, carbon dioxide builds up in the air
    inside the cabin.
    Explain why the rockets also carry a supply of lithium hydroxide.

5. Name the products which would be formed in the reaction between each of
    the following solutions.
    (a) potassium hydroxide and nitric acid
    (b) sodium hydroxide and sulphuric acid
    (c) lithium hydroxide and hydrochloric acid

6. Name the acid and the alkali which could be used to prepare solutions of each of
    the following compounds.
    (a) sodium chloride
    (b) potassium sulphate
    (c) barium nitrate

7. (a) (i) Which gas is produced when a metal carbonate reacts with a dilute
                 acid?
         (ii) Describe the test for this gas.
    (b) Name the products of each of the following reactions.
         (i) calcium carbonate and dilute sulphuric acid
         (ii) sodium carbonate and dilute nitric acid

8. (a) (i) Which gas is produced when a metal reacts with dilute hydrochloric
                 acid?
         (ii) Describe the test for this gas.
    (b) Name the products of each of the following reactions.
         (i) calcium and dilute hydrochloric acid
         (ii) magnesium and dilute sulphuric acid

9. Crystals of magnesium sulphate can be made by adding excess magnesium oxide to dilute sulphuric acid.
   (a) Name the kind of reaction which takes place.
   (b) What happens to the pH of the dilute acid?
   (c) Describe how the excess magnesium oxide can be removed from the solution.

10. An experiment was carried out on a substance **X**.

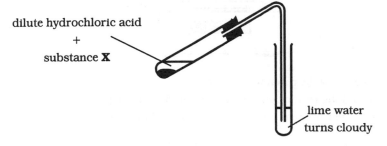

dilute hydrochloric acid
+
substance **X**

lime water
turns cloudy

   (a) Which gas turns lime water cloudy?
   (b) From this experiment, what can be learned about **X**?

11.

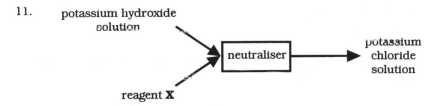

potassium hydroxide
solution

neutraliser

potassium
chloride
solution

reagent **X**

   (a) Name reagent **X**.
   (b) Describe how to produce a dry sample of potassium chloride from the solution.

12. Sodium nitrate and sodium carbonate are both white solids. Given a sample of each, describe a test you could carry out to discover which was which.
   (Give the results of the test.)

13. John spilled sulphuric acid from a car battery on his garage floor. First he poured water over the acid. Then he sprinkled washing soda (sodium carbonate) on it before mopping it up.
   (a) Why did John add water to the acid?
   (b) (i) Name the type of reaction which takes place when washing soda is added to sulphuric acid.
       (ii) Name the gas produced in the reaction.

14. George investigated the reaction of magnesium and dilute hydrochloric acid. Here are his notes.

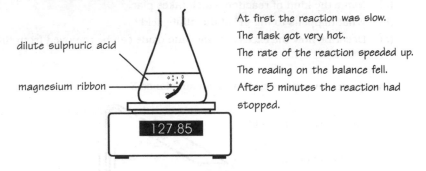

dilute sulphuric acid

magnesium ribbon

127.85

At first the reaction was slow.
The flask got very hot.
The rate of the reaction speeded up.
The reading on the balance fell.
After 5 minutes the reaction had stopped.

(a) Suggest why the reaction speeded up.

(b) Why did the reading on the balance fall during the reaction.

(c) Name the compound of magnesium formed in the reaction.

15. Tom had indigestion caused by too much hydrochloric acid in his stomach. To make himself feel better, he took a Calmo indigestion tablet. The active ingredient in the tablet is magnesium hydroxide.

(a) (i) Which **two** products are formed when magnesium hydroxide reacts with hydrochloric acid.

(ii) Name this kind of reaction.

(c) Calmo tablets are alkaline.

Describe an experiment which could be carried out to show that a Calmo tablet is effective in neutralising acid.

16. Two chemical factories were built close to different rivers. The soap works polluted the West River with sodium hydroxide. The explosives factory polluted the North River with nitric acid.

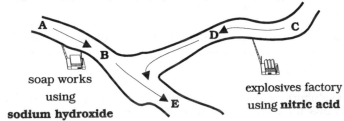

A

B

D

C

soap works
using
sodium hydroxide

E

explosives factory
using **nitric acid**

Government inspectors took water samples from the points **A, B, C, D** and **E**. They tested each sample with pH indicator solution.

(a) Which **two** water samples should be compared to show that the soap works was causing pollution.

(b) The water sample from point **E** was found to be neutral, despite the pollution.

Give a reason for this result.

In answering questions 17 to 22 you may wish to use page 5 of the data booklet.

17. An insoluble product can be formed in the reaction between solutions.
    (a) Name this kind of reaction.
    (b) Identify the insoluble product in each of the following reactions.
        (i) potassium sulphate solution and barium chloride solution
        (ii) calcium chloride solution and sodium sulphate solution

18. (a) Barium carbonate has a solubility of less than $1g\,l^{-1}$.
        (i) From the following list of substances select **two** which together could be used to make barium carbonate:

        barium, barium nitrate, magnesium carbonate,
        carbon, barium oxide, sodium carbonate

        (ii) Describe in detail how you would use these two substances to prepare a dry sample of barium carbonate.
    (b) Which substances are produced when barium carbonate reacts with dilute hydrochloric acid?

19. Stephen investigated the formation of precipitates.
    He added a few drops of sodium sulphate solution to four other solutions.
    All the solutions had a concentration of $1\ mol\ l^{-1}$.

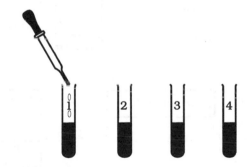

Name of solution	Effect of adding sodium sulphate solution
1. magnesium nitrate	no precipitate
2. calcium nitrate	slight precipitate
3. strontium nitrate	precipitate
4. barium nitrate	precipitate

(a) How would Stephen have been certain that his experiment was fair?
(b) Name the precipitate formed when sodium sulphate was added to a solution of calcium nitrate.
(c) Predict the effect of adding sodium sulphate to a solution of beryllium nitrate.

20. Sodium sulphate solution and barium chloride solution were mixed as shown.

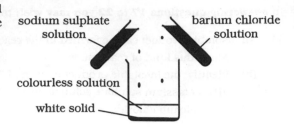

sodium sulphate solution

barium chloride solution

colourless solution

white solid

(a) Name the white solid.

(b) Name the kind of reaction which occurred.

(c) Name the technique which could be used to remove the white solid from the solution.

21. Karen made a solution of table salt (sodium chloride solution). When she added a few drops of the salt solution to silver nitrate solution, a solid formed at the bottom of the beaker.

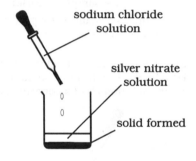

sodium chloride solution

silver nitrate solution

solid formed

(a) What is the name of the solid?

(b) She then added a few drops of the solution to potassium nitrate solution.

Why did **no** solid form at the bottom of the beaker.

22.

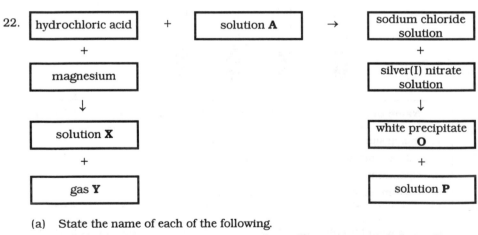

| hydrochloric acid | + | solution **A** | → | sodium chloride solution |

+ +

| magnesium | | silver(I) nitrate solution |

↓ ↓

| solution **X** | | white precipitate **O** |

+ +

| gas **Y** | | solution **P** |

(a) State the name of each of the following.

(i) solution **A**   (ii) solution **X**   (iii) gas **Y**

(iv) white precipitate **O**   (v) solution **P**

(b) State the kind of reaction that occurs when

(i) hydrochloric acid reacts with solution **A**,

(ii) sodium chloride solution reacts with silver(I) nitrate solution.

Credit Level

23. Consider the substances in the grid below.

A sodium hydroxide	B copper(II) oxide	C sodium chloride
D potassium sulphate	E magnesium	F sodium oxide
G carbon	H lithium nitrate	I iron(III) hydroxide
J barium oxide	K zinc	L calcium sulphate

    (a)   Which substances can be classified as salts?

    (b)   Which substances can be classified as bases?

    (c)   Which substances dissolve in water to form alkalis?

24. Chlorine can be prepared in the laboratory by the reaction of concentrated hydrochloric acid with manganese(IV) oxide.

Using **all** the equipment given below, draw a labelled diagram to show how chlorine gas can be produced and collected.

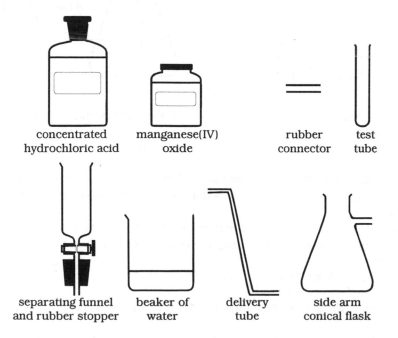

concentrated hydrochloric acid	manganese(IV) oxide	rubber connector	test tube

separating funnel and rubber stopper	beaker of water	delivery tube	side arm conical flask

25. Chromic acid, H_2CrO_4(aq), forms a salt with potassium hydroxide.
    (a) How many moles of potassium hydroxide would be needed to neutralise completely one mole of chromic acid.
    (b) Name the salt formed in the reaction.
        (You may wish to use page 6 of the data booklet to help you.)

26. Jack prepared copper(II) sulphate by adding excess solid copper(II) oxide to sulphuric acid.
    Jill prepared sodium chloride by the addition of sodium hydroxide solution to hydrochloric acid.
    Explain why Jack and Jill used different methods to prepare their salts.

27. Carbon monoxide can be prepared, in a fume cupboard, by passing carbon dioxide over heated carbon.

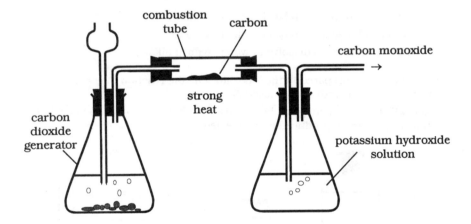

    (a) Explain why potassium hydroxide solution removes unreacted carbon dioxide.
    (b) Draw a suitable arrangement for collecting the carbon monoxide gas.

28. Acid rain attacks limestone in buildings. Carbon dioxide gas is produced.
    It is suggested that painting the limestone would help to resist the attack of acid rain.
    Two paints are to be tested to compare their ability to protect limestone.
    Part of the test includes measuring the volume of carbon dioxide produced in any reaction.
    (a) Draw a clearly labelled diagram of the apparatus that could be used for this test.
    (b) State **two** factors which must be kept the same to make the test fair.

29. During a practical exercise, Yasmin recorded the following notes in her laboratory notebook. She was preparing crystals of blue copper(II) sulphate.

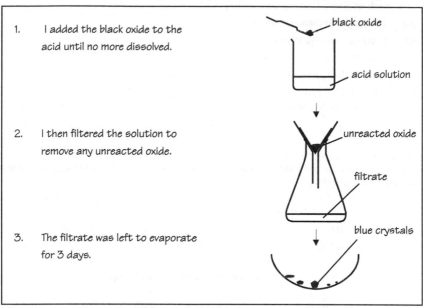

1. I added the black oxide to the acid until no more dissolved.

   black oxide

   acid solution

2. I then filtered the solution to remove any unreacted oxide.

   unreacted oxide

   filtrate

3. The filtrate was left to evaporate for 3 days.

   blue crystals

(a) Name the black oxide and the acid solution.

(b) Name the type of chemical reaction that took place in the beaker.

(c) Name the ion which is coloured blue.

30. Car batteries contain sulphuric acid. The concentration of the acid is to be checked by carrying out a titration. For safety reasons, the battery acid has been diluted to exactly one hundredth of its original concentration.

The grid below contains a number of steps which could be used in the titration.

A add universal indicator solution to the flask	B evaporate to dryness	C measure 10 cm^3 of acid into the flask
D fill burette or syringe with acid	E repeat using smaller additions near the end point, to get a more accurate result	F note volume required for neutralisation
G measure 20 cm^3 of alkali into the flask	H run in acid 1cm^3 at a time shaking the flask after each addititon	I repeat, using same volumes of acid and alkali, but with no indicator

Write down **in the correct order** the letters for the steps which should be used.

In answering questions 31 to 34 you may wish to use page 5 of the data booklet.

31. For each of the following reactions,
    (a) identify the **two** spectator ions,
    (b) rewrite the equations as ionic equations, omitting spectator ions.
       (i) $NaOH(aq) + HCl(aq) \rightarrow NaCl(aq) + H_2O(l)$
       (ii) $AgNO_3(aq) + NaCl(aq) \rightarrow NaNO_3(aq) + AgCl(s)$
       (iii) $2KOH(aq) + H_2SO_4(aq) \rightarrow K_2SO_4(aq) + 2H_2O(l)$
       (iv) $K_2CO_3(aq) + 2HCl(aq) \rightarrow 2KCl(aq) + H_2O(l) + CO_2(g)$
       (v) $CuSO_4(aq) + 2NaOH(aq) \rightarrow Na_2SO_4(aq) + Cu(OH)_2(s)$

32. Sodium hydroxide solution often contains dissolved sodium carbonate as an impurity.This is caused by some of the sodium hydroxide reacting with carbon dioxide from the air.
    The carbonate ions can be removed by adding a few drops of barium chloride solution. The equation for the reaction is:
    $$BaCl_2(aq) + Na_2CO_3(aq) \rightarrow BaCO_3(s) + 2NaCl(aq)$$
    (a) Name an ion which will be an impurity in the final sodium hydroxide solution.
    (b) Rewrite the equation as an ionic equation omitting spectator ions.

33. Patients with stomach problems are given a "barium meal" before being X-rayed. It consists of a suspension of barium sulphate in water.
    This salt can be prepared in the laboratory by a precipitation reaction.
    (a) Name **two** salt solutions which could be mixed to prepare barium sulphate.
    (b) The barium sulphate is separated from the reaction mixture by filtration. If the barium sulphate solution was not washed before it was dried, it would be contaminated.

    Name **two** compounds which could possibly contaminate the barium sulphate sample.
    (c) Barium compounds are toxic.

    Suggest why people can drink "barium meals" without suffering any ill effects.

34. Common salt is extracted from salt mines by pumping in water to dissolve it. The salt solution which is obtained contains magnesium sulphate as an impurity.
    The magnesium ions are removed by adding sodium hydroxide solution.
    $Mg^{2+}(aq) + SO_4{}^{2-}(aq) + 2Na^+(aq) + 2OH^-(aq)$
    $$\rightarrow Mg^{2+}(OH^-)_2(s) + 2Na^+(aq) + SO_4{}^{2-}(aq)$$
    (a) (i) Name the type of reaction taking place between the magnesium sulphate solution and the sodium hydroxide solution.
        (ii) Name the spectator ions in the reaction.
    (b) The products of the reaction can be separated by filtration.
        Draw and label the apparatus you would use in the laboratory to carry out this process.

35. John was given the task of separating copper metal from a mixture containing copper(II) oxide and copper metal. The diagram shows what he did.

chemical substance

mixture of copper(II) oxide and copper metal

solution

solid

solution

solid

Describe in detail how John separated the copper metal from the mixture.

36. Calum added 2.0 cm^3 of sodium hydroxide solution to 25.0 cm^3 of hydrochloric acid. He noted the temperature rise.

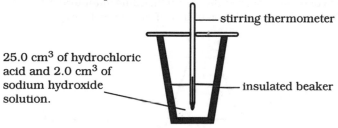

stirring thermometer

25.0 cm^3 of hydrochloric acid and 2.0 cm^3 of sodium hydroxide solution.

insulated beaker

He then repeated his experiment using different volumes of the sodium hydroxide solution. Calum's results are shown in the table.

Temperature rise / °C	Volume of added sodium hydroxide solution / cm^3
1.6	2.0
3.7	4.0
6.0	6.0
8.4	8.0
10.2	10.0
11.9	12.0
11.8	14.0
11.0	16.0
9.6	18.0

(a) Explain why the temperature rises in each of the experiments.

(b) Draw a **line graph** of his results

(c) What volume of sodium hydroxide solution was needed to neutralise the hydrochloric acid?
You may wish to refer to your graph.

(d) Calum carried out a second set of experiments using more concentrated sodium hydroxide solution.

How would the volume of sodium hydroxide solution needed to neutralise the acid have compared with your answer to part (c)?

37. (a) What volume of hydrochloric acid (concentration 0.1 mol l^{-1}) is required to neutralise 50 cm^3 of sodium hydroxide solution (concentration 0.2 mol l^{-1})?

   (b) What is the concentration of sulphuric acid if 50 cm^3 are neutralised by 25 cm^3 of potassium hydroxide solution (concentration 1 mol l^{-1})?

   (c) What volume of nitric acid (concentration 2 mol l^{-1}) is required to neutralise 20 cm^3 of sodium hydroxide solution (concentration 0.5 mol l^{-1})?

   (d) What is the concentration of hydrochloric acid if 12.6 cm^3 neutralises 20 cm^3 of potassium hydroxide solution (concentration 0.1 mol l^{-1})?

   (e) What is the concentration of sulphuric acid if 17.3 cm^3 neutralises 25 cm^3 of sodium hydroxide solution (concentration 0.5 mol l^{-1})?

38. Iain determined the mass of iron present in a piece of wire.

   Step 1. He completely reacted the wire with dilute sulphuric acid. This produced a solution of iron(II) sulphate, $FeSO_4$.

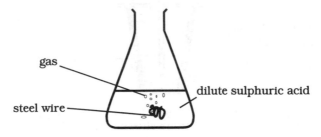

   Step 2. He found the volume of potassium permanganate solution needed to react with the iron(II) sulphate solution by titration.

   (a) Why was the wire reacted with sulphuric acid in Step 1?

   (b) Name the gas formed in Step 1.

   (c) Iain found that 20.2 cm^3 of potassium permanganate solution, concentration 0.15 mol l^{-1}, were needed to react with the iron(II) sulphate solution.

      (i) How many moles of potassium permanganate were needed to react with the iron(II) sulphate solution.

      (ii) **One** mole of potassium permanganate reacts with **five** moles of iron(II) sulphate.

      Calculate he mass of iron present in the steel wire.

39. Hard water forms a scum with soap. This hardness can be caused by dissolved calcium ions.

   Klenzmore is a soap company which tests hardness of different water samples.

   The samples are titrated with an acid called EDTA, using a suitable indicator.

   One mole of calcium ions reacts with **one** mole of EDTA.

   In one titration 18.6 cm^3 of 0.12 mol l^{-1} EDTA reacted with 25.0 cm^3 of a water sample.

   Calculate the concentration of calcium ions, in mol l^{-1}, in the sample.

40. Stuart wanted to prepare ammonium sulphate.

He added 0.5 mol l^{-1} sulphuric acid from a burette to 20 cm^3 of 0.5 mol l^{-1} ammonia solution in a conical flask with pH indicator.

The equation for the reaction is:

$$2NH_3(aq) + H_2SO_4(aq) \rightarrow (NH_4)_2SO_4(aq)$$

(a) Calculate the volume of sulphuric acid Stuart used to neutralise the ammonia solution.

(b) The indicator was remove from the ammonium sulphate solution by filtering the solution through charcoal.

How would Stuart then obtain a sample of solid ammonium sulphate from the solution?

41. Sodium hypochlorite is a substance present in household bleaches. It gives them their bleaching action.

The concentration of sodium hypochlorite in a bleach can be found by adding an excess of dilute hydrochloric acid to a measured sample of the bleach. The acid reacts with the sodium hypochlorite and the volume of chlorine given off is measured.

$$NaOCl(aq) + 2HCl(aq) \rightarrow NaCl(aq) + H_2O(l) + Cl_2(g)$$

In an investigation of three different household bleaches, the following results were obtained.

Bleach	Volume of bleach used /cm^3	Volume of chlorine produced /cm^3
A	6	100
B	9	150
C	4	90

(a) Find, **by calculation**, which bleach contains most sodium hypochlorite per litre.

(b) Some cleaners contain acid.
     Why should such cleaners not be used with bleach?

Topic 10   Making Electricity

General Level

1. One of the most widely used batteries is known as the dry cell. This is used in portable radios, torches and toys.

    (a) What energy change always takes place when a dry cell is used?

    (b) Explain why the dry cell eventually has to be replaced.

    (c) What is the purpose of the ammonium chloride paste in the dry cell?

    (d) Explain why the ammonium chloride is in the form of paste and not completely "dry".

    (e) State **one** advantage of a nickel-cadmium battery compared to a dry cell.

2. The battery in a car is an example of a battery which can be recharged.

    (a) Name the kind of battery which is in a car.

    (b) What energy change takes place during recharging?

3. Many portable radios can use electricity from the mains as well as from batteries.

    (a) State **one** advantage of having a radio which has batteries.

    (b) In the house, is it cheaper to run the radio from the mains or the batteries?

4. A simple cell can be made up using a lemon and two different metals.

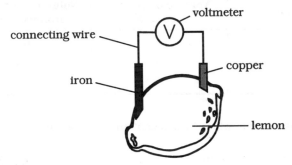

    (a) The lemon juice is an electrolyte.

    What is the purpose of an electrolyte in a cell?

    (b) Clearly state the direction of the electron flow through the wire.

    (c) What would happen to the reading on the voltmeter if the iron was replaced with a piece of zinc?

5. When magnesium ribbon is added to copper sulphate solution, the ribbon starts to break up at the surface, a brown solid forms, and the solution eventually becomes colourless.

    Magnesium ribbon does not react with sodium sulphate solution.

    Explain these observations.

6. A simple dry cell can be made from everyday materials.

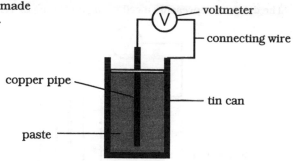

The paste is made from salt (sodium chloride), water and porridge.
Porridge is composed mainly of starch.

(a) Clearly state the direction in which electrons flow through the wire.

(b) Name the electrolyte in the paste.

(c) Why could sugar **not** be used as an electrolyte?

(d) Would the voltage be higher or lower if an aluminium can were used?

7. The arrangement shown below is used to produce a flow of electrons.

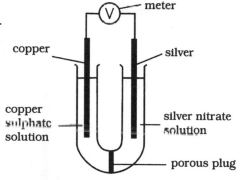

(a) In which direction do the electrons flow through the meter?

(b) Explain your answer.

8. (a) Using magnesium, copper, magnesium sulphate solution and copper sulphate solution, state what **A**, **B**, **C** and **D** must be to give a flow of electrons in the direction shown

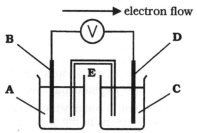

(b) (i)   What is **E** on the diagram known as?

(ii) Why is it necessary?

(iii) Why is sodium chloride solution suitable but sugar solution is **not**?

9. The diagram represents a cell giving a reading of 1.1 volts.

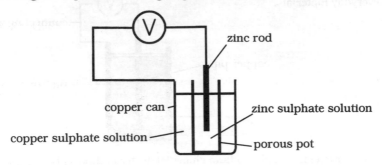

(a) State the direction of electron flow through the meter.

(b) What difference would there be in the meter reading if the zinc was replaced by magnesium and the zinc sulphate solution by magnesium sulphate solution?

(c) If the cell shown was allowed to run for 24 hours, what visible signs of a chemical change would there be?

10. Refer to the diagram.

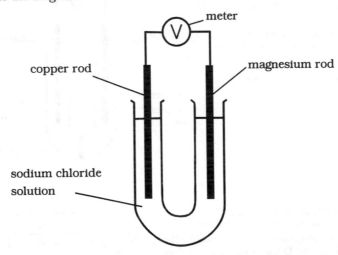

(a) (i) In which direction do the electrons flow through the meter?

(ii) Explain your answer.

(b) Name a metal which could replace magnesium and produce a flow of electrons in the opposite direction through the meter.

(c) What would happen to the meter reading if the copper rod was replaced by an iron rod?

(d) (i) What would happen to the meter reading if the sodium chloride solution was replaced by sugar solution?

(ii) Explain your answer.

11. James put a copper coin into silver nitrate solution. The coin turned a grey colour.

He the put the coin into sodium chloride solution. The coin did not change in any way.

Explain what was observed in each case.

12. The Italian professor, Alessandro Volta, made one of the first batteries. It was called a "Voltaic pile". The following diagram shows the pile connected to a meter for measuring current.

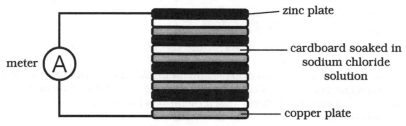

(a) When the sodium chloride solution is replaced by potassium nitrate solution, a reading is still obtained on the meter. When ethanol is used, no reading is obtained.

Explain each of these results.

(b) What will happen to the reading on the meter if the zinc is replaced by tin?

13.

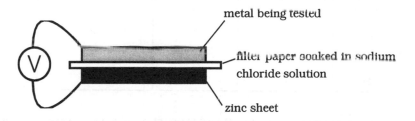

Three metals were tested in the experiment above.
The results are shown in the table.

Metal tested	Voltage / V	Direction of electron flow
R	0.3	zinc to metal R
S	0.4	metal S to zinc
T	1.0	zinc to metal T

(a) State which **one** of the four metals (**R,S,T** and zinc) is highest in the electrochemical series.

(b) Arrange the four metals in order of their position in the electrochemical series, with the highest first.

Credit Level

14. (a) State whether or not a reaction takes place when each of the following metals is added to the solution.
    (i) magnesium added to copper(II) sulphate solution
    (ii) copper added to sodium chloride solution
    (iii) zinc added to silver nitrate solution
    (iv) copper added to zinc sulphate solution
    (v) silver added to copper(II) chloride solution
    (vi) aluminium added to magnesium nitrate solution

    (b) Write ion-electron equations for the reactions which occur.

15. A pupil carried out a series of experiments involving the displacement of one metal by another. Four different metals were used and two of them, **P** and **Q** were from unlabelled bottles. Each metal was placed, in turn, in various metal salt solutions.

    The following table shows the results of the experiments. A tick ($\sqrt{}$) indicates that a displacement reaction was seen to occur; a cross ($\times$) that no reaction occurred.

Metal	Solutions			
	zinc sulphate	lead nitrate	copper(II) chloride	silver nitrate
magnesium	$\sqrt{}$	$\sqrt{}$	$\sqrt{}$	$\sqrt{}$
copper	$\times$	$\times$	$\times$	$\sqrt{}$
P	$\times$	$\sqrt{}$	$\sqrt{}$	$\sqrt{}$
Q	$\sqrt{}$	$\sqrt{}$	$\sqrt{}$	$\sqrt{}$

(a) Suggest names for metals **P** and **Q** which would give the results shown in the table.

(b) (i) What would have been the colour of the solution after the copper had reacted with the silver nitrate solution?

   (ii) For this reaction, write the ion-electron equation to show how the copper would have changed.

16. A piece of zinc is added to copper(II) chloride solution.
    (a) State what happens
       (i) to the piece of zinc,
       (ii) to the copper(II) ions,
       (iii) to the colour of the solution.
    (b) Write ion-electron equations for the oxidation and reduction reactions which occur.

17. Part of the electrochemical series is shown opposite.

    From its position in the series, state what would
    happen when metal **X** is added to an aqueous
    solution of

    (a) copper(II) sulphate,

    (b) magnesium chloride.

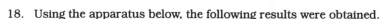

| magnesium |
| metal **X** |
| iron |
| tin |
| copper |

18. Using the apparatus below, the following results were obtained.

filter paper soaked in sodium
chloride solution

test metal

copper block

Test metal	Voltmeter reading / V
lithium	2.9
sodium	2.4
magnesium	1.6
iron	0.5
tin	0.4
copper	0.0
silver	-0.4

   (a) What name is given to this kind of series of metals arranged from voltmeter
        readings?

   (b) Explain why magnesium ribbon does **not** react with sodium sulphate
        solution

   (d) Suppose the copper block was replaced by a block of tin.

        (i)   What would be the reading on the voltmeter if the test metal is iron?

        (ii) What would be the reading on the voltmeter if the test metal is silver?

        (iii) Which metal could be used as the test metal to give a voltmeter reading
              of approximately 1.2 V?

19.

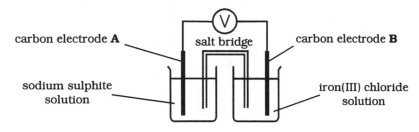

carbon electrode **A**   salt bridge   carbon electrode **B**

sodium sulphite
solution

iron(III) chloride
solution

    In the cell shown, the electrons flow through the meter from electrode **A** to
    electrode **B**.

    (a) State the electrode at which

         (i) oxidation takes place,   (ii) reduction takes place.

    (b) Write the ion-electron equation for the reaction involving the sulphite ions at
         electrode **A**.

    (c) Explain what happens in the salt bridge.

20.

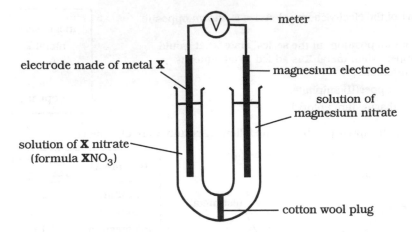

electrode made of metal **X**

magnesium electrode

solution of magnesium nitrate

solution of **X** nitrate (formula **X**NO_3)

meter

cotton wool plug

Oxidation takes place at the magnesium electrode.

(a)   In which direction will electrons flow through the meter?
(b)   Write the ion-electron equation for the reaction at the magnesium electrode.
(c)   Which electrode will decrease in mass?
(d)   Write the ion-electron equation for the reaction at electrode **X**.

21.

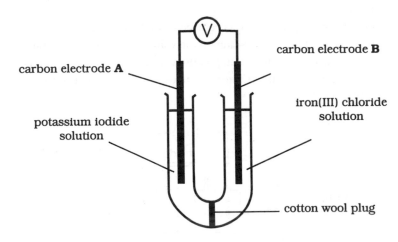

carbon electrode **B**

carbon electrode **A**

potassium iodide solution

iron(III) chloride solution

cotton wool plug

The reaction occuring at electrode **B** is:
$$Fe^{3+}(aq) + e^- \rightarrow Fe^{2+}(aq)$$

(a)   Name the type of chemical reaction occurring at electrode **B**.
(b)   In which direction do the electrons flow through the meter?
(c)   What product will be formed from iodide ions at electrode **A**?
(d)   Write the ion-electron equation for the reaction at electrode **A**.

22. Bill wanted to show that chemicals can be used to produce an electric current.

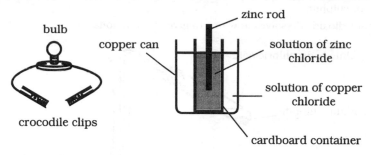

zinc rod

bulb

copper can

solution of zinc chloride

solution of copper chloride

crocodile clips

cardboard container

When the crocodile clips were attached to certain parts of the apparatus, the bulb lit.

(a) State clearly where the crocodile clips should have been attached.

(b) In a second experiment, the cardboard container was replaced by a glass beaker.

Explain why the bulb did not light.

23. Pure nickel can be obtained by the electrolysis of nickel(II) chloride solution.

(a) Write the ion-electron equation for the formation of the nickel.

(b) Is this an example of oxidation or reduction?

(c) Does this reaction occur at the positive or negative electrode?

24. Some hearing aid batteries contain silver(I) oxide. Silver can be extracted from the silver oxide in spent batteries using a two step process.

Step 1 involves reacting the silver(I) oxide with nitric acid to form silver(I) nitrate solution.

Step 2 is shown in the following diagram.

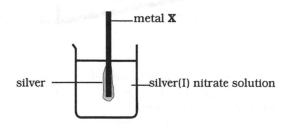

metal X

silver

silver(I) nitrate solution

(a) The reaction in step 2 is an example of a redox reaction.

Give another name for the kind of reaction occurring at this step.

(b) Write the ion-electron equation for the reduction reaction.

(c) No silver is produced if the metal X is platinum.

What does this indicate about the reactivity of platinum?

25. Sulphur dioxide gas can be produced if dilute hydrochloric acid is added to sodium sulphite.

Sulphur dioxide dissolves in water to give sulphite ions.

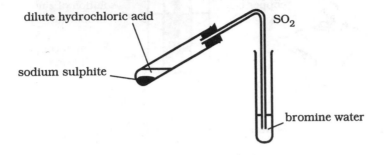

The bromine water is decolourised.

(a) Name the kind of reaction which occurs between bromine and sulphite ions.

(b) (i) Write the ion-electron equation to show what happens to the bromine.

(ii) Write the ion-electron equation to show what happens to the sulphite ions.

26.

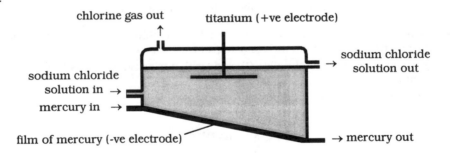

The cell shown is used for the industrial manufacture of chlorine.

(a) In the cell, the sodium chloride is broken up by the electrical energy. What name is given to this process?

(b) Name the kind of reaction which occurs at the mercury electrode.

(c) Write the ion-electron equation for what happens at the titanium electrode.

(d) Suggest an advantage in maintaining a continuous flow of sodium chloride solution.

27. Sodium sulphite solution reacts with bromine solution. The sulphite ions are oxidised. The ion-electron equation for the oxidation reaction is:

$$SO_3^{2-}(aq) + H_2O(l) \rightarrow SO_4^{2-}(aq) + 2H^+(aq) + 2e$$

This reaction takes place in the cell shown.

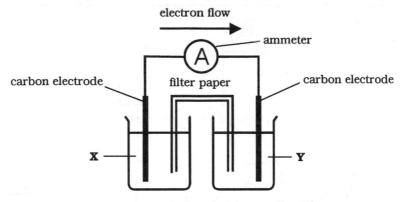

(a) On the diagram, identify the two solutions at **X** and **Y** so that the flow of electrons is in the direction shown.

(b) What is the purpose of the filter paper soaked in electrolyte between the beakers?

(c) In the reaction, the bromine solution is reduced.

Write the ion-electron equation for this reaction.

(d) If samples of the two solutions were mixed, what would you see happening?

28. Copper can be purified by electro-refining. This process is illustrated in the diagram.

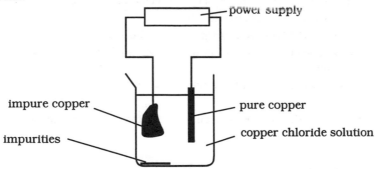

The ion-electron equation for the process occurring at the impure electrode is:

$$Cu(s) \rightarrow Cu^{2+}(aq) + 2e$$

(a) What name is given to the kind of reaction at the impure electrode?

(b) Is the impure electrode the positive or the negative electrode?

(c) During electro-refining, what happens to the mass of the pure copper electrode?

(d) Write the ion-electron equation for the reaction at the pure copper electrode.

29. Nicola was given a chemistry set as a birthday present. One of the activities was to use electricity from a chemical reaction to operate a digital stop clock.
Nicola was able to make the stop clock work using only the items shown in the diagram.

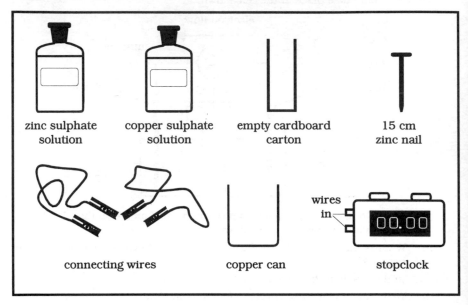

zinc sulphate solution   copper sulphate solution   empty cardboard carton   15 cm zinc nail

connecting wires   copper can   wires in   stopclock

(a) Draw a labelled diagram to show how Nicola arranged the items to make the experiment work.

(b) Nicola stirred the copper sulphate solution with an iron screwdriver.

   (i) What colour would Nicola have seen on the blade of the screwdriver?

   (ii) What caused this to take place?

   (iii) Write the ion-electron equation for this change.

(c) Nicola repeated the stirring of the copper sulphate solution with a piece of aluminium.

Suggest why there was **not** a reaction in this case.

30. Copper(II) chloride solution is electrolysed in the apparatus shown.

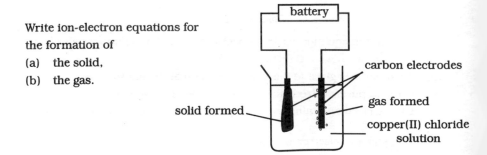

Write ion-electron equations for the formation of

(a) the solid,

(b) the gas.

battery

carbon electrodes

gas formed

copper(II) chloride solution

solid formed

31. Electrochemical cells use redox reactions to produce electricity. An example of a cell is shown.

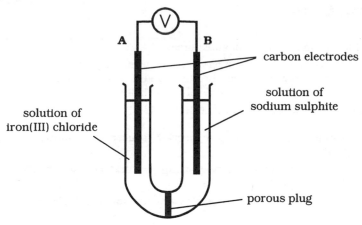

The reaction taking place at electrode **B** of the above cell is:

$$SO_3^{2-}(aq) + H_2O(l) \rightarrow SO_4^{2-}(aq) + 2H^+(aq) + 2e$$

(a) Name the type of reaction taking place at electrode **B**.

(b) Clearly state the direction of electron flow through the meter.

(c) As the reaction proceeds, iron(III) ions react to form iron(II) ions. Explain why this happens.

(d) Write the ion-electron equation for the reaction at electrode **A**.

32. The following passage is taken from a journal on industrial chemistry. It contains information about some important chemicals which can be obtained from common salt.

"When salt solution is electrolysed, hydrogen, chlorine and sodium hydroxide are obtained. These electrolysis products are put to a wide variety of uses, some of which are outlined below.

The chlorine product, together with hydrocarbons from crude oil, is used to make PVC plastic and solvents. The sodium hydroxide product is used in the manufacture of paper from wood pulp.

Two of the electrolysis products, the sodium hydroxide and the hydrogen, are used along with vegetable oils to make soap and margarine respectively."

(a) Present the information given in the passage in a suitable way.

(b) The following reactions take place at the electrodes when the solution of common salt is electrolysed.

positive electrode: $2Cl^-(aq) \rightarrow Cl_2(g) + 2e$

negative electrode: $2H_2O(l) + 2e \rightarrow H_2(g) + 2OH^-(aq)$

   (i) Name the type of reaction taking place at the negative electrode.

   (ii) As the electrolysis continues, explain what will happen to the pH of the salt solution.

Topic 11   Metals
General Level

1. Consider the following list of substances:

    gold foil, hydrogen gas, molten iron, sulphur powder,
    magnesium ribbon, bromine liquid, calcium granules,
    liquid oxygen, phosphorus sticks, copper foil.

    Which of the substances conduct electricity?

2. Aluminium metal is used to make aircraft, saucepans, window frames and
    cooking foil.

    Copper metal is useful for making wiring, hot and cold water pipes and the
    bases of cooking pans.

    For each metal state **three** properties which make it suitable for the use to which
    it is put.

3. This country recycles many important metals.
    (a) What is meant by the recycling of metals?
    (b) Explain why there is a need to recycle many metals.

4. (a) Name **three** metals which are stored under oil.
    (b) What does this indicate about the reactivity of these metals?

5. Steel for different uses can be made by adding different metals to iron.

    Titanium is added to make steel suitable for use in rockets. Magnets are made
    from a steel which contains cobalt. The steel for railway lines is made by adding
    manganese to iron. Drill bits require a very hard steel. This is made by adding
    tungsten to the iron.

    Present the above information in a table with suitable headings.

6. The apparatus shown can be used to compare the reactivity of different metals.

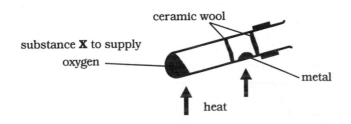

    (a) What is the name of substance **X**, used to supply oxygen on heating?
    (b) How can this experiment be used to compare the reactivity of different
        metals?

7. The following experiments were set up to investigate the rate of reaction of four metals, **P**, **Q**, **R** and **S**, with dilute hydrochloric acid.

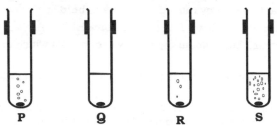

P   Q   R   S

(a) Place the four metals in order of reactivity. (Start with the most reactive.)

(b) State **three** factors which must be kept the same for the comparison to be a fair one.

(c) (i) Which gas is produced in the reaction of a metal with dilute hydrochloric acid?

(ii) Name the other product in the reaction of magnesium with hydrochloric acid.

8. When sodium metal is added to cold water, the metal melts to form the shape of a ball and quickly moves about the surface of the water. Hydrogen gas is rapidly produced and sodium hydroxide solution is formed.

(a) How can the gas be identified?

(b) Explain why the metal melts.

(c) Name a metal which reacts more vigorously than sodium with water.

9. Over 60 different metals occur in the earth and we have found uses for almost all of them.

Gold has been known since the earliest civilisation. It is too soft to make into tools but is used to make jewellery and coins.

Copper was discovered about 4000 BC. It is one of the best conductors of electricity, which makes it a good choice for electrical wiring. Its lack of reactivity makes it a good choice for making hot or cold water pipes.

About 1000 BC, iron was first extracted from its ores. Its hardness makes it very useful, and when converted to steel it is the raw material for cars, ships, railway lines and machinery.

The first of the modern metals to be discovered was aluminium, in 1825. This light metal does not corrode to a large extent. Aircraft, window frames, milk bottle tops and wrapping foil are all made from aluminium.

Present the above information in a table with four headings.

10. The earliest people on earth used gold and silver for making jewellery. Other metals like sodium and magnesium were unknown until approximately 200 years ago.

(a) Explain why gold and silver were among the first metals to be discovered.

(b) Explain why sodium and magnesium were **not** discovered until recent times.

11. Some metals are found **uncombined** in the earth's crust but most have to be extracted from their **ores**.
    (a) Explain what is meant by each of the terms in **bold**?
    (b) Name **two** metals which are found uncombined.
    (c) What can be concluded about the reactivity of metals which are found uncombined?
    (d) Name a metal that can be extracted from its ore by heating with carbon.

12. A pupil carried out some experiments with iron oxide, sodium oxide and silver oxide. On heating the three metal oxides, it was found that one decomposed to form the metal and oxygen gas. On heating with carbon, one of the other two metal oxides reacted to form the metal.
    (a) Which metal oxide would decompose on heating alone?
    (b) Which metal oxide would **not** decompose on heating with carbon?

13. Iron is produced from ore by a process called smelting. The chemical reactions take place in a huge tower.
    (a) What name is given to the tower?
    (b) The following reactions take place in the tower.
        Write a word equation for each.
        (i)   the burning of the coke
        (ii) the production of carbon monoxide gas
        (iii) the formation of iron from the ore

14. Alloys can be made with very specific properties. Some are very hard, some are resistant to corrosion and some have special magnetic or electrical properties.
    (a) What is meant by an alloy?
    (b) Name **three** alloys and give a use for each.
    (c) Explain why two aluminium/copper alloys can have different strengths.

15. Wire gauzes in laboratories can be made to last longer by using an alloy of iron.
    (a) Why are alloys of metals made?
    (b) Suggest **two** properties that make iron a good choice for a wire gauze.

16. Steel is an alloy of iron and carbon. The table shows how two properties of steel change as the percentage of carbon is increased.

Percentage of carbon	Hardness	Strength
0.00 - 0.15	low	high
0.16 - 0.25	medium	high
0.26 - 0.50	high	medium
0.51 - 1.50	high	low

    (a) State how the hardness of steel changes as the percentage of carbon is increased.
    (b) Predict the **two** properties of a steel containing 1.7% carbon.

17. One use of alloys is for hip joint replacements.

    These alloys do not react easily with body fluids.

    The material chosen for a hip joint replacement must have other properties.

    Suggest **two** such properties.

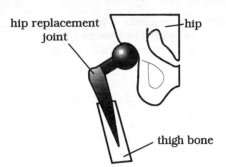

hip replacement joint

hip

thigh bone

18. Solders are alloys of lead (melting point 327 °C) and tin (melting point 232 °C). The table shows the melting points of solders containing different proportions of tin.

Percentage of tin in solder (by mass)	Melting point / °C
10	305
20	280
30	260
40	240
50	215
60	190
70	190
80	200
90	215

(a) Draw a **line graph** of melting point against percentage of tin in solders.

(b) State the percentage of lead present in the solder with the lowest melting point.

(c) Solders which do not contain lead are made. They are used to solder pipes for drinking water.

    Suggest why this has been done.

19. Caesium can be produced by heating a mixture of calcium and caesium chloride to 750 °C.

$$Ca + 2CsCl \rightarrow CaCl_2 + 2Cs$$

(a) State whether caesium would be formed as a solid, liquid or gas in this reaction.
    (You may wish to use page 3 of the data booklet to help you.)

(b) Caesium must be stored in the absence of water and air.

    Suggest a reason for this.

Metals

20. The reactivity of halogens were compared by passing them as gases over heated iron wool.

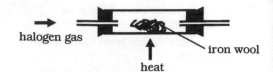

halogen gas

heat

iron wool

The results were as follows.

Halogen	Reaction with heated iron wool
Chlorine	The iron wool glows brightly even when the heat is removed.
Bromine	The iron wool gives an orange glow, but only while being heated.
Iodine	The iron wool gives a dull glow, but only while being heated.

(a) What would you expect to see when fluorine is passed over heated iron wool?

(b) Name the compound formed.

21. Read the following passage.

"Magnesium reacts readily with acids and oxygen.

Aluminium might be expected to behave in a similar way. However, if you test aluminium, you will often find that this is not the case. This is mainly due to a layer of aluminium oxide forming very rapidly when the metal is first exposed to air.

This oxide layer does not flake off or allow air and water to pass through it. It is this layer which prevents further corrosion of the aluminium."

Which of the following would be the most suitable title for the passage?

    A   Reactions of metals   **B**   Reactions with air

    C   The oxidation of metals   **D**   The reactivity of aluminium.

22. Consider the following statements about the reactions between selected metals and air.

"Nickel is relatively inert to corrosion at ordinary temperatures. It burns, producing its oxide (NiO), when roasted in air.

Cobalt is not affected by air at room temperature. However, when the temperature is raised, it forms a surface layer of oxide.

Strong heating of manganese brings about the following reaction, which does **not** occur under normal conditions.

$$3Mn(s) \ + \ 2O_2(g) \ \rightarrow \ Mn_3O_4(s)$$

Chromium burns well only at temperatures well over 2000 K. Below this temperature it is unreactive."

Use the information to write out **two** general statements which could be applied to **all** of the four metals.

23. Some magnesium ribbon was added to dilute hydrochloric acid in a test tube. Bubbles of gas were given off, quite slowly at first, but more quickly after a few seconds. The contents of the test tube became warmer.

The following five statements are all true.

A   During the reaction, acid is used up, so fewer $H^+(aq)$ ions are left.

B   Reactions speed up when the temperature increases.

C   The magnesium has a thin oxide layer which first reacts with the acid.

D   Magnesium reacts slowly with water as well as with acid.

E   Magnesium reacts more quickly with acid than do most other metals.

Which **two** statements can be used to explain why the bubbles of gas were given off more quickly after a few seconds than at the very start of the reaction.

24. Nuclear reactors can overheat and become very dangerous.
Liquid sodium can be used to cool down reactors. It flows round the reactor in pipes.

(a)   Suggest why sodium is used rather than iron.

You may wish to use page 3 of the data booklet to help you.

(b)   Suggest why sodium is used rather than water.

Credit Level

25. The oxides of metals **X** and **Y** are unaffected by heat but the oxide of **Z** gives off oxygen when it is heated. The oxide of **Y** is stable to heating with carbon but the oxide of **X** decomposes.

    (a) Place the three metals in order of reactivity. (Start with the most reactive.)

    (b) Suggest a name for each of the metals **X**, **Y** and **Z**.

26. A pupil was asked to investigate three metal oxides **LO**, **M_2O** and **NO**. On heating strongly, **LO** broke down into a metal **L** and oxygen. The other two oxides did not break down.

    (a) From this evidence what can be deduced about the reactivity of metal **L**?

    (b) How could you test **M_2O** and **NO** in order to find out which was the more reactive of the metals **M** and **N**?

27. Carbon monoxide can be used to extract iron from iron(III) oxide.
    Carbon dioxide is produced in the reaction.

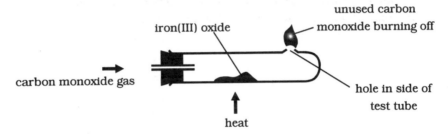

    (a) Name the type of reaction which takes place.

    (b) Explain why calcium cannot be extracted from its oxide in this way.

28. The cells which power heart pacemakers contain lithium metal.

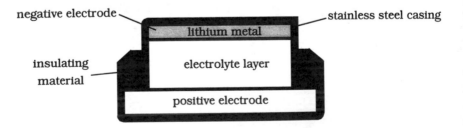

    (a) Explain why lithium metal is a good choice for the negative electrode.

    (b) What is the purpose of the electrolyte layer in the cell?

    (c) Explain why water is **not** used in the electrolyte layer.

29. Uranium metal is obtained from ores containing uranium(IV) oxide and uranium (VI) oxide. The extraction of the metal involves three steps.

1. The oxide is converted to uranium(VI) fluoride.

2. The uranium(VI) fluoride is reduced by hydrogen.

$$UF_6(g) \ + \ H_2(g) \ \xrightarrow{100\,°C} \ UF_4(s) \ + \ 2HF(g)$$

3. The uranium(IV) fluoride is reduced by magnesium metal.

$$UF_4(g) \ + \ 2Mg(s) \ \xrightarrow{1600\,°C} \ U(l) \ + \ 2MgF_2(l)$$

Using the information above

(a) state **two** facts that can be concluded about the melting point of uranium(IV) fluoride,

(b) state whether uranium is a more active or less active metal than magnesium.

30. The results of experiments with four metals **W**, **X**, **Y** and **Z** and their compounds are summarised in the table below.

Metal	Column 1 Reaction of metal with dilute acid	Column 2 Action of heat on metal oxide	Column 3 Reaction of metal with cold water
W	hydrogen evolved	no reaction	hydrogen formed
X	no reaction	no reaction	no reaction
Y	hydrogen evolved	no reaction	very slow reaction
Z	no reaction	metal formed	no reaction

(a) State what information about the order of reactivity of the metals can be obtained from

(i)   Column 1 alone,

(ii) Column 2 alone.

(b) Now use **all** the information to put the metals into an order of reactivity placing the most active first.

(c) Suggest a name for each metal **W**, **X**, **Y** and **Z**.

31. **A, B, C** and **D** are four metals to be arranged in an order of reactivity.

(a) In each of the cases (i) to (iv) state which of the two metals is more reactive.

(i)   The oxide of **C** does **not** decompose on heating, while that of **A** does.

(ii) **B** reacts with dilute acid to produce hydrogen gas; **D** does **not**.

(iii) When **D** is added to a solution containing ions of the metal **A**, **A** is displaced and **D** dissolves.

(iv) **C** reacts readily with cold water, **B** reacts slowly with steam.

(b) Use the above information to place the four metals in order of reactivity. (Start with the most reactive.)

32. Some information about the metals **M, E, T, A** and **L** and their compounds is listed below.

    (i) With water, **A** reacts vigorously, **M** slowly, **E, T** and **L** do **not** react.

    (ii) **T** displaces **E** from a solution containing ions of **E**.

    (iii) Carbon reduces the oxides of **E** and **T** but **not** the other oxides.

    (iv) **M, A** and **L** react with dilute hydrochloric acid while **T** and **E** do **not**.

    (a) For each bit of information (i) to (iv), what can be concluded about the relative reactivity of the metals?

    (b) Use the above information to place the five metals in order of reactivity (most reactive first).

    (c) When nitrates of these metals are heated only one decomposes to give the metal. Which is most likely to do so?

33. Calculate the simplest (empirical) formula for the following compounds from the percentage composition by mass.

    (a) 75% carbon, 25% hydrogen

    (b) 27% carbon, 73% oxygen

    (c) 25% magnesium, 75% chlorine

    (d) 33% calcium, 27% sulphur, 40% oxygen

34. An analysis of a chloride of titanium gave the following results.

    Mass of titanium = 4g ; Mass of chlorine = 12g

    What is the simplest formula for the chloride?
    (Take the relative atomic mass of titanium as 48.)

35. An analysis of an oxide of vanadium gave the following results.

    Mass of vanadium = 5g ; Mass of oxygen = 4g

    What is the simplest formula for the oxide?
    (Take the relative atomic mass of vanadium as 50.)

36. A compound of phosphorus and sulphur is used to make match heads.
    A sample weighing 11g is found to contain 4.8 g of sulphur.
    What is the simplest formula for the compound?

37. 4g of a hydrocarbon was shown on analysis to contain 3g carbon.
    What is the simplest formula for the hydrocarbon?

38. 36g of an oxide of copper was strongly heated and carbon monoxide gas was passed over it. When the oxide was completely reduced, 32g of copper was left.
    What is the simplest formula for the oxide?

39. A container when empty had a mass of 60g. An oxide of lead was added and the mass of the container plus the oxide was 120g. Carbon monoxide gas was then passed over the heated oxide and after complete reduction the mass of the container plus lead metal was 112g.
    What is the simplest formula for the oxide?

Topic 12   Corrosion

General Level

1. Each year corrosion costs our country millions of pounds.
   (a) Explain what is meant by corrosion.
   (b) What special term is applied to the corrosion of iron?
   (c) Consider this list of substances:

   glass, magnesium, sandstone, sulphur, zinc,
   calcium carbonate, sodium, aluminium, plastic, calcium

   Copy the table and place each of the substances in the appropriate column.

Substances which corrode	Substances which do not corrode

2. (a) Apart from iron, what **two** substances are necessary for rusting to occur?
   (b) When iron rusts, what happens to the iron atoms?

3. Acid rain is common in industrial areas.
   How does acid rain affect the rate of corrosion of metals?

4. Three test-tubes were set up as shown.

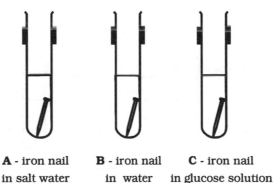

A - iron nail   **B** - iron nail   **C** - iron nail
in salt water   in water   in glucose solution

Ferroxyl indicator was added to each of the tubes. On inspection it was found that the nail in tube **A** had corroded most. The amount of corrosion in tubes **B** and **C** was much the same.
   (a) How does ferroxyl indicator help to compare the rates of corrosion?
   (b) Explain why salt in the water speeds up the rate of corrosion whereas glucose does not.

5. A pupil set up the following experiment.

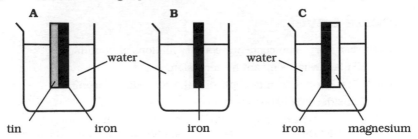

(a) In which experiment would the corrosion of iron be fastest?

(b) Explain your answer.

6. Explain each of the following.

    (a) A ship corrodes faster at sea than on a fresh-water loch.

    (b) The hulls of ships often have blocks of magnesium attached to them.

    (c) It is inadvisable for a plumber to attach copper piping to an iron storage tank.

    (d) Iron railings which are painted corrode less rapidly than unpainted railings.

    (e) It is inadvisable for a plumber to use solder containing lead to join copper pipes.

    (f) A motor car body is often connected to the negative terminal of the car battery.

    (g) Scrap magnesium can be used to protect underground storage tanks but scrap copper **cannot** be used.

7. The experiment shown was carried out to investigate the rusting of iron.

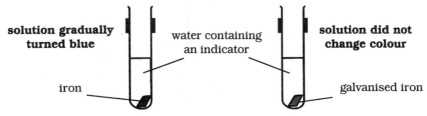

(a) Suggest a name for the indicator used.

(b) Explain what is meant by galvanised iron.

(c) Why does galvanised iron hardly rust even when badly scratched?

8. Both zinc and tin are used to protect iron and steel containers from corrosion.

    Metal dustbins are made from iron which has been dipped into molten zinc; cans for food are tin-plated.

    (a) What name is given to the process of coating iron with zinc?

    (b) Explain why zinc is preferred to tin for protecting dustbins.

9. Two corrosion experiments with iron nails are shown.

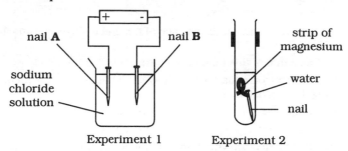

Experiment 1   Experiment 2

(a) In experiment 1, which nail, **A** or **B**, will be protected against rusting?

(b) In experiment 2, how does the magnesium protect the nail from rusting?

(c) For each of these experiments describe how the method is actually used to protect iron or steel on a large scale.

10. Oil rigs, made of iron and steel, corrode readily at sea.

State **one** method which could be used to help prevent corrosion of oil rigs and explain briefly how the method works.

11. Galvanising could be said to provide 'double protection' against corrosion of iron.

This is because the process provides both physical protection and electrochemical protection.

Explain whether or not a coating of copper instead of zinc would be as effective in providing

(a) physical protection,

(b) electrochemical protection.

12. **X** and **Y** are two metals. When each is attached to iron only **Y** decreases the speed of rusting of iron.

(a) Which metal is more reactive, **X** or **Y**?

(b) Which metal would be most effective in sacrificially protecting iron?

13. Both silver and gold are used to cover objects made of steel. As well as providing an attractive finish, the steel is protected against corrosion.

(a) What name is given to the process of coating steel with silver or gold?

(b) Explain why the coating protects the iron against corrosion.

14. Equipment used by Scott in his expedition to the South Pole nearly eighty years ago has been found recently. It shows very little sign of rusting.

Explain why iron rusts so slowly when the temperature is below 0 °C.

15. Steel can be protected from rusting by coating it with other substances. One method is dipping it in molten plastic.

(a) Why does coating steel with plastic prevent rusting?

(b) Chromium plated steel rusts quickly if scratched.

What does this tell you about the reactivity of chromium?

Credit Level

16. Corrosion involves atoms at the surface of a metal losing electrons and changing to metal ions.

    (a) State the name of this kind of reaction.

    (b) Write ion-electron equations to show what happens to the metal atoms during the corrosion of

        (i) iron,   (ii) zinc,

        (iii) magnesium,   (iv) aluminium.

    (c) Write the ion-electron equation to show what can happen to the iron(II) ions which are formed during the corrosion of iron.

    (d) Write the ion-electron equation to show how hydroxide ions are formed during corrosion of a metal.

17. Two experiments are set up as shown.

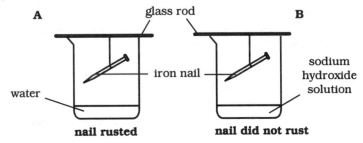

A   glass rod   **B**

iron nail

sodium hydroxide solution

water

nail rusted   **nail did not rust**

Explain why the nail in experiment **B** did not rust.

18. Acid mists lead to faster corrosion of metals.

    (a) Write ion-electron equations for each of the reactions which occur when iron is corroded by acid.

    (b) Explain why galvanising does **not** protect iron permanently from corrosion by acid.

19. Three experiments were set up outside to investigate the corrosion of "tin" cans. These cans are made of iron which has been coated with tin.

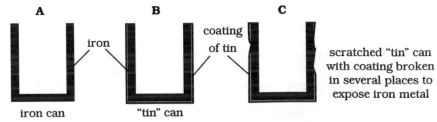

A   **B**   **C**

iron   coating of tin

scratched "tin" can with coating broken in several places to expose iron metal

iron can   "tin" can

    (a) (i) In which experiment will the iron not rust?

        (ii) Explain your answer.

    (b) (i) In which experiment will the iron rust fastest?

        (ii) Explain your answer.

20. Consider the following cells.

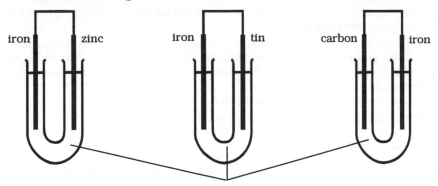

gel containing ferroxyl indicator plus an electrolyte

(a) Name the ion which reacts with ferroxyl indicator to produce
   (i) a blue colour,
   (ii) a red colour.
(b) What colour, if any, will be observed at each of the electrodes in the three cells?
(c) Write the ion-electron equation to show the reaction at each electrode in the three cells
(d) What is the direction of electron flow in each of the cells?

21. Archaeologists found some corroded silver coins and a badly rusted sword.
   (a) The silver coins were restored by wrapping them in zinc foil in a beaker of salt solution.
       What type of reaction took place?
   (b) The iron blade was attached to its handle by a copper band.
       Explain why, although the copper was uncorroded, the iron had rusted badly.

22. Dental amalgam is a mixture of metals including mercury, silver and tin. The amalgam slowly corrodes in the mouth. Corrosion is more rapid if the amalgam makes contact with a gold filling in a neighbouring tooth.
   Explain why contact with gold increases the rate of corrosion of the dental amalgam.

23. In the 19th century, Humphrey Davy suggested that the Royal Navy could protect the copper sheeting on the hulls of its ships from corrosion by attaching small patches of iron to them.
   (a) Write the ion-electron equation to show what happens to the atoms when copper corrodes.
   (b) Explain why attaching patches of iron would have prevented the copper from corroding.

24. "OLD COPPER BOTTOM"

"Old Copper Bottom" was the nickname of William Forbes of Stirling, who lived during the 18th century.

Forbes made his fortune by buying up all the available copper in the country when he heard rumours that the Navy was planning to experiment with copper sheeting on the hulls of its wooden warships. He sold the copper to the Navy at a large profit and when the experiment failed because of the use of iron nails, he bought the copper back at a lower price.

Forbes then pointed out the obvious fact that copper nails should have been used. After this he was able to resell the copper to the Admiralty, and made a second large profit.

Explain why it is "obvious" that copper nails and **not** iron nails should have been used in the experiment.

Topic 13   Plastics and Synthetic Fibres
General Level

1. Nylon is a synthetic fibre; wool is a natural fibre.
    (a) Explain the difference between a natural and a synthetic fibre.
    (b) What is the raw material from which most synthetic fibres are made?
    (c) State **two** uses for nylon.
    (d) State an advantage of a synthetic fibre as against a natural fibre.
    (e) State a disadvantage of a synthetic fibre as against a natural fibre.

2. The following is a list of plastics:
    polystyrene, polythene, polyvinyl chloride (PVC), perspex, melamine, bakelite
    (a) Copy and complete the following table by matching each plastic with the
         appropriate uses.

Plastic	Uses
	washing-up bowls, waste-bin liners
	window frames, pipes, guttering
	plates, tumblers
	safety screens, spectacle lenses
	electric plugs and switches
	packaging, ceiling tiles

    (b) Give **one** reason why each plastic is used in a particular way.

3. Many items which were once made of other materials are now made of plastic.
    However, plastics can also have disadvantages.
    (a) State **two** reasons why plastics are now preferred for pipes and guttering.
    (b) State **two** problems which can arise from the use of plastics.

4. Explain the purpose of each of the following.
    (a) the Teflon skin on some frying pans
    (b) the PVC skin on some wallpapers
    (c) the PVC covering of electric wire

5. Thermosetting plastics have different properties from thermoplastics.
    (a) Explain what is meant by
         (i)   a thermosetting plastic,
         (ii) a thermoplastic.
    (b) Give **two** examples of each.

6. Plastics are examples of polymers. Different monomers are used to make different plastics.

    (a)   Explain what is meant by

        (i) a monomer,

        (ii) a polymer.

    (b)   Name the process which takes place when a polymer is made from a monomer.

    (c)   Name the polymer which is made from

        (i) styrene,

        (ii) propene,

        (iii) vinyl chloride.

    (d)   What is common to the structures of all of the above monomers?

    (e)   The above monomers are obtained from the same raw material.

        (i) What is this raw material?

        (ii) Name the **two** processes by which the monomers are obtained from the raw material.

7. Poly(ethene) is a widely used polymer.

    (a)   (i)   Name the monomer unit.

        (ii)   Draw the full structural formula for the monomer unit.

    (b)   Draw the structure of part of a poly(ethene) chain to show how **three** monomer units have joined together.

8. A plastic bottle has the following label.

> **NON-BIODEGRADABLE**
> To dispose of this plastic bottle,
> simply fill with hot water. When soft,
> empty and flatten.

    (a)   Explain what is meant by non-biodegradable.

    (b)   What type of plastic is suggested by the instructions on the label?

9.

$$\begin{array}{ccc} H & & H \\ | & & | \\ C & = & C \\ | & & | \\ H & & CN \end{array} \quad \text{acrylonitrile}$$

    (a)   (i)   Name the polymer made from acrylonitrile

        (ii)   The polymer can be melted and forced through tiny holes to form acrylic fibres.

           What term is used to describe a polymer which can be melted and reshaped?

    (b)   Why are the fumes from burning plastics dangerous?

10. The following passage contains information about polymers.

"Most plastics can be made by a variety of processes. One common method is the solution method where the monomer is dissolved in a suitable solvent. This is used for high density poly(ethene), poly(propene), and poly(phenylethene).

Poly(phenylethene), along with polyesters, polyamides and low density poly(ethene) can also be made by the bulk method where the monomer is the reaction fluid.

Another method uses the monomer emulsified in water. This emulsion method is used for poly(chloroethene), poly(tetrafluoroethene), and poly(buta-1,3-diene).

Finally, in the fluid catalysed bed method, used for poly(ethene) and poly(propene), the gaseous monomer flows through the solid catalyst."

Draw a table with columns to present this information.

11. There are various types of plastics. Each type has a variety of uses.

Polyurethane can be used for lagging hot water pipes. One of the main uses of poly(ethene) is for packaging food. Poly(propene) can be used to make shoe heels. Another plastic called polyamide can be used to make machine parts. Light plastic drinking cups are often made of polystyrene.

Choose suitable headings and present the above information in a table.

Credit Level

12. Many plastics burn or smoulder to give off toxic fumes.

    Name a plastic which can give off

    (a) carbon monoxide,

    (b) hydrogen chloride,

    (c) hydrogen cyanide.

13. Polymers can be classified depending on how the monomers join together.

    (a) Explain the difference between an addition and a condensation polymer.

    (b) Look at the following list of polymers:

    > poly(ethene), bakelite, poly(chloroethene), nylon

    From the list, name

    (i) a condensation polymer which is a thermoplastic,

    (ii) a condensation polymer which is thermosetting,

    (iii) an addition polymer which contains only two elements.

14. PTFE is an addition polymer made from tetrafluoroethene.

    (a) What does PTFE stand for?

    (b) Draw the full structural formula for tetrafluoroethene.

    (c) Draw the structure of part of a PTFE chain to show how **three** monomer units have joined together.

15. Poly(propene) is used to make many kitchen items.

    (a) (i) Name the monomer unit.

    (ii) Draw the full structural formula for the monomer unit.

    (b) Draw the structure of part of a poly(propene) chain to show how **three** monomer units have joined together.

16. Perspex is as transparent as glass but does not break easily. This polymer is therefore used to make safety screens, spectacle lenses and aeroplane windows. The following diagram shows part of a molecule of perspex.

    (a) Draw the structural formula for the repeating unit in perspex.

    (b) Draw the structural formula for the monomer used to make perspex.

    (c) What type of polymerisation takes place when perspex is produced from the monomer?

17. Orlon is a synthetic fibre made from monomers with the following structure.

$$
\begin{array}{cc}
H & H \\
| & | \\
C = & C \\
| & | \\
H & CN
\end{array}
$$

(a) Draw the structural formula for the repeating unit in Orlon.

(b) Draw the structure of part of the Orlon chain to show how **three** monomer units have joined together.

18. Polyvinylidene chloride is an addition polymer. It is added to carpet fabrics to reduce flammability. It is made from the monomer vinylidene chloride.

Part of the polymer chain is shown.

$$
\begin{array}{cccccc}
H & Cl & H & Cl & H & Cl \\
| & | & | & | & | & | \\
-C- & C- & C- & C- & C- & C- \\
| & | & | & | & | & | \\
H & Cl & H & Cl & H & Cl
\end{array}
$$

(a) What is meant by an **addition** polymer?

(b) How many repeating units are shown ?

(c) Draw the full structural formula of the vinylidene chloride monomer.

(d) State a problem associated with the burning of polymers.

(e) Many polymers are **not** biodegradable.
Why might this be an advantage?

19. Poly(butene) is used to make pipes which carry hot water under pressure. This is very useful in plumbing and underfloor heating

(a) Poly(butene) is made using the following monomer.

$$
\begin{array}{cccc}
H & H & H & H \\
| & | & | & | \\
C = & C- & C- & C-H \\
| & | & | & \\
H & & H & H
\end{array}
$$

Draw the part of the poly(butene) chain which is formed by **three** monomer units linking together.

(b) The butene monomer shown has a number of isomers.
Draw an isomer which

(i) could also be used to form a polymer,

(ii) could **not** be used to form a polymer.

Topic 14   Fertilisers
General Level

1. Fertilisers are compounds which restore to the soil the essential elements for plant growth.

    (a) Name **three** elements which are restored to the soil through use of fertiliser.

    (b) Explain why woodland growth does **not** require the use of fertilisers while farm-land requires the use of large quantities of fertilisers.

2. The flow chart shows part of the nitrogen cycle.

    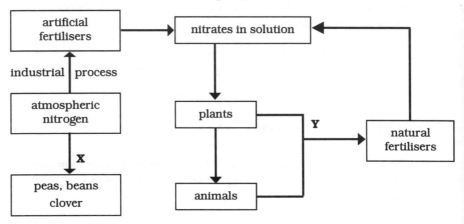

    (a) Explain what is meant by
        (i)   an artificial fertiliser,
        (ii) a natural fertiliser.

    (b) Give an example of each.

    (c) What is process **X** called?

    (d) What types of living thing act on dead material to bring about process **Y** ?

    (e) Why is it often necessary to add fertilisers to the cycle?

    (f) Give **one** example of an environmental problem that can be caused by the use of artificial fertiliser.

3. Information about some common fertilisers is given in the following table.

Name	Formula	Solubility in water
X	$(NH_4)_3PO_4$	dissolves easily
Y	KNO_3	dissolves easily
urea	$CO(NH_2)_2$	dissolves slowly

    (a) Name compounds **X** and **Y**.

    (b) What properties of **X** and **Y** make them suitable as fertilisers?

    (c) Why is urea particularly suitable as a fertiliser in very wet countries?

4. The graph shows how the level of nitrates in the soil of a farmer's field varied throughout a particular year.

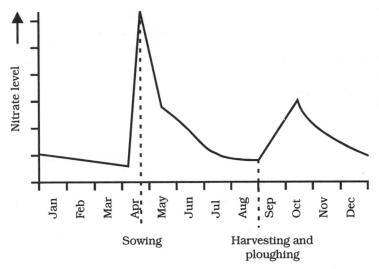

Sowing

Harvesting and ploughing

(a) Suggest why the level of nitrates increased in April.

(b) Suggest why the level of nitrates decreased from April to August.

(c) During periods of heavy rain, nitrates from the soil are washed into rivers. What effect does this have on the rivers?

5. At the turn of the century, a team of scientists led by Fritz Haber discovered a cheap way to make an important compound for the fertiliser industry.

This is now called the Haber Process.

(a) Name the compound which Haber produced.

(b) Which catalyst is used for the reaction?

(c) State **two** other conditions which are necessary for a successful yield of the compound.

(d) Suggest why the pipes used in this industrial process have thick walls.

6. Ammonium nitrate fertiliser can be made by the NITRAM Process as shown.

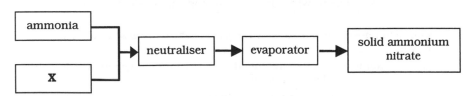

(a) Write the formula for ammonia and ammonium nitrate.

(b) Name **X**.

7. Ammonia solution can be made from ammonia.
    (a) Describe the smell of ammonia.
    (b) State the effect of ammonia solution on pH paper.
    (c) Name the process used in industry to manufacture ammonia.

8. A flash of lightning through the air can result in the combustion of nitrogen and oxygen.
    (a) Name the product of this reaction.
    (b) Why does the process occur during lightning storms?
    (c) Draw the apparatus that can be used to simulate this reaction in the laboratory.
    (d) State **two** effects on the soil of rain water which falls during lightning storms.

9. The manufacture of nitric acid is an important process in the chemical industry.

    (a) What name is given to this process?
    (b) Name gas **Z**.
    (c) State the kind of chemical reaction taking place in the first stage of the process.
    (d) What role does the platinum play?

10. Nitrate fertilisers are made from nitric acid.

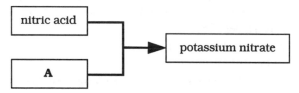

    (a) Name reagent **A**.
    (b) Name the other product of this reaction.
    (c) Name the kind of reaction which is taking place.
    (d) State **two** reasons why nitrate compounds are useful fertilisers.

11. Potassium phosphate contains two elements which are essential for plant growth.
    (a) (i) Name an element not found in potassium phosphate which plants require in large amounts.
        (ii) Name a compound which gardeners could use to supply this element.
    (b) Compounds which are used as fertilisers contain elements that are essential for plant growth. They must also have a particular property.
        State this property.

12. The graph shows the masses of three elements used to make synthetic fertilisers between 1900 and 1990.

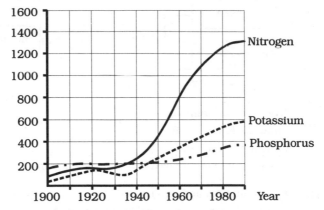

Mass of element / 10^3 tonnes

(a) In which year were equal masses of nitrogen and phosphorus fertilisers made?

(b) What trend is shown by the graph for the use of all three elements between 1940 and 1990?

(c) Name a synthetic fertiliser containing potassium and nitrogen as well as oxygen.

(d) Calcium phosphate is readily available but cannot be used directly in fertilisers.

Suggest why it is unsuitable.

You may wish to use page 5 of the data booklet.

13. A chemistry class was studying the movement of molecules in gases.

The experiment shown was set up.

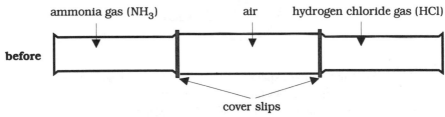

ammonia gas (NH₃)   air   hydrogen chloride gas (HCl)

before

cover slips

The cover slips were removed.
After a time, a white solid, ammonium chloride, formed.

white solid (ammonium chloride)

after

(a) Explain why the white solid appeared.

(b) What does the position of the white solid indicate about the movement of ammonia gas compared to hydrogen chloride gas?

14. The diagram shows how ammonia is made industrially.

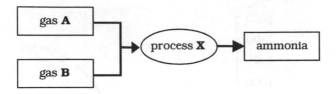

(a) Give a use for ammonia.
(b) Name gas **A** and gas **B**.
(c) Name industrial process **X**.
(d) How is ammonia removed from the reaction mixture?

15. Air contains nitrogen and oxygen.
Nitrogen dioxide can be produced by sparking air.

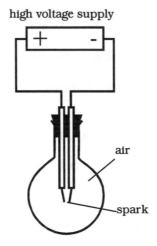

(a) Why is a high voltage spark needed to produce nitrogen dioxide?
(b) When does this process take place naturally?
(c) Nitrogen dioxide is also produced by car engines.
Why does this speed up the rusting of car exhausts?

Credit Level

16. (a) Why do farmers add lime (calcium oxide) to their fields?

    (b) Explain why ammonium sulphate fertiliser should not be added at the same time.

17. The data below refers to the formation of ammonia by the Haber process.

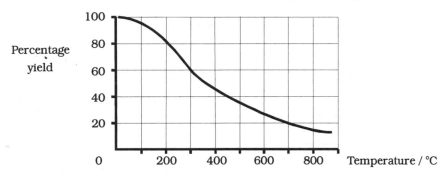

    (a) Name the elements which are necessary for the manufacture of ammonia.

    (b) From the information given above, what happens to the yield as the temperature is increased?

    (c) Explain why the reaction is carried out at a moderately high temperature.

    (d) Explain why the yield of ammonia is not 100%.

18. (a) Name a substance that could be added to ammonium nitrate to release ammonia.

    (b) Using your answer to (a), write the balanced chemical equation for the reaction.

    (c) Using your answer to (a), write the ionic equation for the reaction.

19. An experiment was carried out as shown.

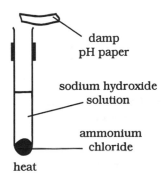

    (a) State the colour to which the pH paper would turn,

    (b) Name the gas which was produced.

20. (a) Ammonium nitrate is very soluble in water and this allows essential elements to be taken in by the roots of crop plants very quickly.

Suggest why the compound's solubility can also be a disadvantage in its use as a fertiliser.

(b) Ammonium phosphate is another important fertiliser.

Name a compound which will react with ammonium phosphate to produce ammonia.

21. The flow diagram below shows some of the stages in the industrial manufacture of nitric acid.

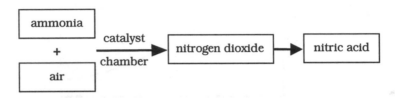

(a) Why is nitrogen dioxide made from ammonia and **not** from nitrogen?

(b) Explain why the reaction in the catalyst chamber is carried out at a moderately high temperature.

(c) (i) Is it necessary to continue heating the catalyst chamber throughout the process?

(ii) Explain your answer.

22. A student carried out two experiments on compound **X**.

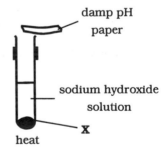

Experiment 1

dilute sulphuric acid

X

heat

A colourless gas was given off and the limewater became milky.

Experiment 2

damp pH paper

sodium hydroxide solution

X

heat

A gas was given off which turned the pH paper blue.

(a) Name the gas given off in Experiment 1.

(b) Name the gas given off in Experiment 2.

(c) Name compound **X**.

23. Some plants can convert atmospheric nitrogen into nitrogen compounds.
    This is called fixing nitrogen.
    Scientists are trying to develop cereal crops which fix nitrogen.
    (a) Explain why some plants are able to fix nitrogen.
    (b) Why would the development of cereal crops which fix nitrogen save on
        energy costs?
    (c) Name the **industrial** process which is used to fix nitrogen.

24. Ammonia is manufactured in industry by the Haber Process. In this process, the
    percentage yield of ammonia varies with pressure.

    The graph shows the percentage yield against pressure, at 350 °C.

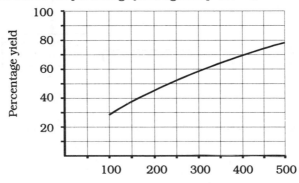

    (a) (i) Copy the graph and add a second curve to show how the percentage
            yield would vary with pressure at a higher temperature.
        (ii) Why is this reaction carried out at 350 °C and **not** at 450 °C?
        (iii) How is ammonia removed from the reactant gas?
    (b) Name **two** chemicals which could be used to produce ammonia in the
        laboratory

25. In the manufacture of ammonia by the Haber Process, the reactant gases are
    compressed from a pressure of 25 atmospheres to 200 atmospheres. This raises
    the temperature so the mixture of gases is cooled before it enters the catalytic
    converter.
    (a) Suggest why the temperature of the gases is lowered before entering the
        catalytic converter.
    (b) Reactions take place on the surface of a catalyst. A catalyst can be produced
        in pellets of different shapes.

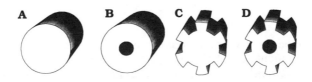

    Explain which of the shapes **A**, **B**, **C** or **D** would be best for use as a catalyst.

26. The flow chart refers to an industrial chemical complex.

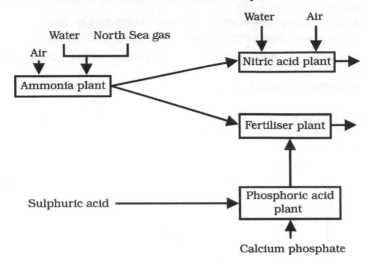

(a) Air and water are used as raw materials because they are readily available.

Suggest **one** other reason why they are used as raw materials.

(b) Which reactant for the ammonia plant must be produced in the reaction between North Sea gas and water?

(c) The nitric acid is produced when nitrogen dioxide dissolves in water.

(i) Name the industrial process which converts ammonia into nitrogen dioxide.

(ii) Name the catalyst used.

(d) Name the salt formed in the fertiliser plant.

27. Lawn sand contains ammonium sulphate and iron(II) sulphate. One compound improves grass growth, the other is present to kill moss.

contains
ammonium sulphate
iron(II) sulphate

(a) Name the ion which is present in lawn sand to kill moss.

(b) Ammonium sulphate is made from ammonia.

Name the chemical which reacts with ammonia to form ammonium sulphate.

28. Heating a mixture of solid ammonium sulphate and sodium hydroxide pellets produces ammonia gas. Ammonia reacts with iron oxide.

Draw a diagram to show apparatus you would set up to make ammonia gas and to pass it over hot iron oxide.

In your diagram label the apparatus and chemicals used.

29. Calculate the percentage (by mass) of each of the elements present in the following compounds.

    (a) SO_2 (b) CH_4

    (c) MgO   (d) $CuSO_4$

    (e) sodium hydroxide   (f) potassium sulphate

    (g) calcium carbonate   (h) magnesium nitrate

30. Urea, $CO(NH_2)_2$, ammonium sulphate, $(NH_4)_2SO_4$ and ammonium nitrate, NH_4NO_3, are three fertilisers that supply nitrogen.

    Find the most useful fertiliser by calculating the percentage mass of nitrogen in each.

31. Ammonium phosphate, $(NH_4)_3PO_4$, is a synthetic fertiliser.

    (a) Calculate the mass of nitrogen in 100 g of ammonium phosphate.

    (b) Calculate the mass of phosphorus in 1 kg of the fertiliser.

Topic 15   Carbohydrates and Related
General Level   Substances

1. The diagram represents the process by which energy is produced in animals.

    (a) Name the process.
    (b) Name gases **X** and **Y**.
    (c) Give **three** examples of how the energy produced can be used by animals.

2. A spoonful of sugar is burned in air. It is then placed in a jar of oxygen.
    (a) What difference will be observed in the burning?
    (b)   (i) What are the products of the reaction?
           (ii) Describe tests which would enable you to identify each of the products.
          (iii) In addition to the above products what else is produced in this
                 experiment?

3. Plants make glucose by photosynthesis.

    (a) Identify gases **X** and **Y**.
    (b) To which family of compounds
         does glucose belong?
    (c) Name the substance, stored in
         plants, which is made when
         glucose units join together.

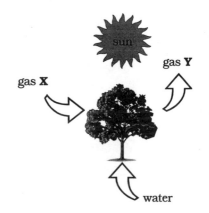

4. Carbohydrates are energy containing foods.
    (a) Where does this energy come from?
    (b) Write a word equation to show what happens when glucose combines with
         oxygen in our bodies.

5. The flow diagram below shows an important process which occurs in green plants.

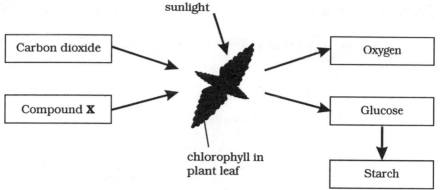

(a) Name the process.
(b) What is the purpose of the chlorophyll?
(c) Name compound **X**.
(d) What kind of reaction occurs in the change from glucose to starch?

6. The flow chart shows part of the carbon cycle.

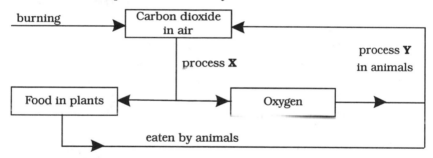

(a) (i) Name process **X**.
    (ii) Name process **Y**.
(b) The amount of carbon dioxide entering the air has increased considerably in the last 50 years.

    Suggest a reason for this increase.
(c) In recent years, many countries have cleared extensive areas of forest for the development of towns and industry.

    Explain why this presents dangers to life on earth.

7. Starch and glucose are both carbohydrates.
(a) Name the elements which are found in a carbohydrate.
(b) Why does glucose dissolve easily in water and yet starch does not?
(c) Explain what is seen when a beam of light is passed through
    (i) glucose solution,
    (ii) starch in water.

Carbohydrates and Related Substances

8. (a) A carbohydrate was tested as shown in the diagram below.

Test 1

solution of carbohydrate
+Benedict's (or Fehling's)
solution

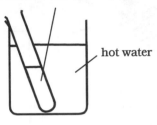

hot water

Result: No change in colour of Benedict's (or Fehling's) solution.

Test 2

iodine solution

carbohydrate

Result: Iodine solution did not change colour.

Suggest a name for the carbohydrate which was tested.

(b) A different carbohydrate was tested as shown below.

Test 3

carbohydrate in water
+dilute hydrochloric acid

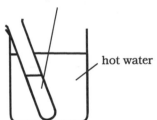

hot water

Result: After the solution was neutralised, Benedicts (or Fehling's) solution gave an orange precipitate.

Test 4

iodine solution

carbohydrate

Result: Iodine solution turned blue/black.

(i) Name the carbohydrate used in Tests 3 and 4.

(ii) Name the carbohydrate produced by the reaction in Test 3.

(iii) What kind of substance, present in saliva, could have been used in place of the dilute hydrochloric acid to produce the same result as in Test 3.

9. Glucose, sucrose and starch are all white solids.

Given an unlabelled sample of each, describe how you would discover which was which.

(Give the results of the tests that you would carry out.)

10. Carbohydrates supply the body with energy.

    Explain why eating a Mars bar (containing glucose) just before a race might be of more value to a sportsman that eating bread (containing starch).

11. Alcohol for drinks can be made from carbohydrates.

    (a) Name this process.

    (b) Name **three** sources of carbohydrates for the production of an alcoholic drink.

    (c) Describe briefly how to obtain a sample of alcohol from carbohydrates.

12. Study the flow diagram below and answer the questions which follow.

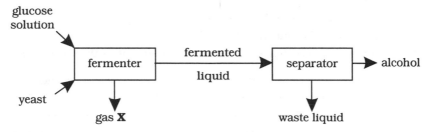

    (a) Name gas **X** .

    (b) What kind of substance, present in yeast, acts as a catalyst for the reaction?

    (c) Name the alcohol produced by this process.

    (d) How is the alcohol separated from the waste liquid?

13. The flowchart shows some of the many chemicals obtained from wood.

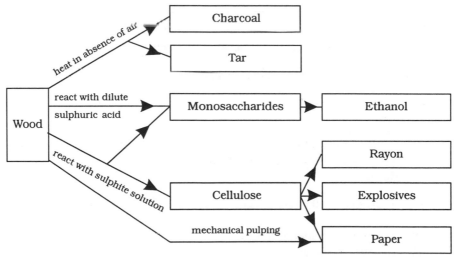

    Use the flowchart to

    (a) name the compound which is made from wood and used to make rayon,

    (b) name the type of **chemical** treatment of wood that is the first stage in paper making.

Carbohydrates and Related Substances   127

Credit Level

14. Consider this list of sugars:

    glucose, maltose, fructose, sucrose

    (a) Name the isomer of
        (i) glucose,
        (ii) maltose.
    (b) Which sugar does **not** give a positive result to the Benedict's (Fehling's) test?

15. Many of the foods we eat contain starch. The starch molecules are hydrolysed in our bodies.
    (a) Explain what is meant by hydrolysis.
    (b) What is formed by the hydrolysis of starch?
    (c) Why do foods containing glucose give us energy faster than starch foods?

15. A compound **X** is thought to be a carbohydrate. It is tested as follows.

    Test 1   When burned in air, **X**   produced CO_2 and H_2O
    Test 2   When **X** is added to iodine solution, there is no change in colour.
    Test 3   When **X** is warmed with Benedict's solution, there is no change in colour.
    Test 4   After **X** has been heated with dilute acid, the product gives a positive Benedict's test.

    (a) From Test 1 **alone**, explain whether it is reasonable to conclude that **X** is a carbohydrate.
    (b) From Test 2 **alone**, what conclusion can be reached?
    (c) From Test 3 **alone**, what conclusion can be reached?
    (d) (i) In Test 4, what is happening to **X** when it reacts with acid?
        (ii) What name is given to this kind of reaction?

17. A glucose molecule can be represented as shown.

$$HO - \boxed{G} - OH$$

    (a) Use the representation to draw **three** units in the starch polymer chain.
    (b) What kind of polymerisation take place when starch is formed from glucose?

18. The production of ethanol from glucose is normally carried out at a temperature around 40 °C.
    (a) Write the molecular formula for glucose.
    (b) (i) Would the reaction be speeded up by boiling?
        (ii) Explain your answer.
    (c) Explain why there is a limit to the concentration of ethanol obtained in this reaction.

19. Polylactic acid is a biodegradable plastic which can be made form lactic acid.
    The diagram shows how molecules of lactic acid join together.

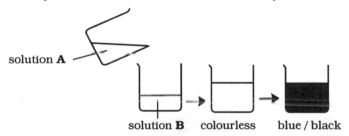

polylactic acid

(a) Copy the part of the structure of polylactic acid and continue the chain to
    show how **three** monomer units join together.
(b) Suggest a name for this kind of polymerisation.

20. Some magicians use chemical reactions in their acts.
    In one such reaction, two colourless solutions, **A** and **B,** are added together. After
    a time delay, the colourless reaction mixture suddenly turns blue / black.

solution **A**

solution **B**   colourless   blue / black

(a) Name **two** substances which could have reacted together to give the
    blue / black colour.
(b) To prepare for his act, a magician needed to know how the concentration of
    solution **A** affected the time it took for the colour to appear.
    He did four experiments, each with a different concentration of solution **A**.
    In each experiment, he measured the time it took for the blue / black colour
    to appear.

    State **two** factors which the magician had to keep the same in his
    experiments.

21. Bees collect nectar from flowers to make honey. The nectar contains sucrose
    which is broken down in the bees' bodies to give glucose and fructose.
    (a) Name the family of compounds to which glucose and fructose belong.
    (b) Name the type of substance in the bees' bodies which can break down
        sucrose.
    (c) Describe the test you would use to show that honey contains glucose.

Carbohydrates and Related Substances   **129**

Formulae, Equations and Calculations Based on Equations

Formulae

General Level

1. Write the chemical formula for each of the following substances.

   (a)

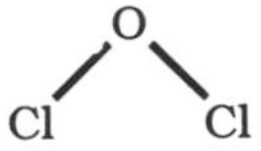

   (b) H — H

   (c)

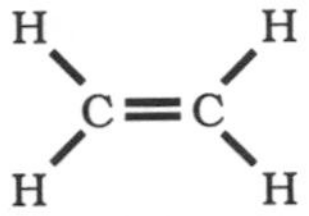

   (d)

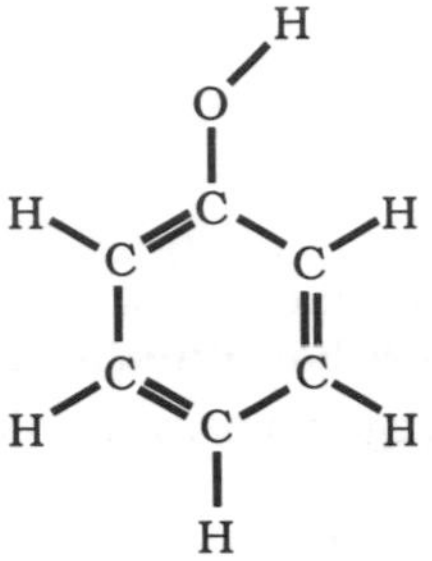

   (e)

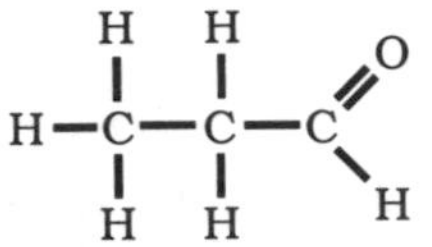

2. The molecules below show the way atoms are arranged in different molecules. Choose a name for each substance from the following list:

   chlorine,   hydrogen oxide,   carbon chloride,   nitrogen,
   hydrogen chloride,   nitrogen hydride,   oxygen

   (a)

   (b)

   (c)

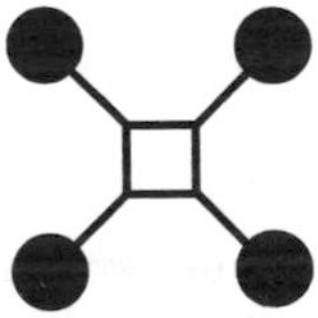

   (d)

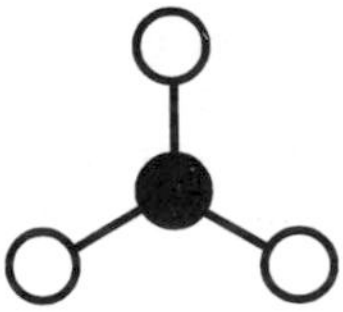

   (e)

   (f)

   (g)

3. Write the chemical formula for each of the following compounds.

   (a) sulphur trioxide   (b) carbon dioxide
   (c) carbon monoxide   (d) silicon tetrafluoride
   (e) phosphorus pentachloride (f) uranium hexafluoride

4. Write the chemical formula for each of the following compounds.
   (a) hydrogen oxide
   (b) phosphorus fluoride
   (c) nitrogen chloride
   (d) hydrogen iodide
   (e) sulphur chloride
   (f) silicon oxide

5. Write the state symbol to show whether each of the following substances is a solid, liquid, gas, or in aqueous solution.
   (a) hydrogen gas
   (b) liquid nitrogen
   (c) solid carbon
   (d) solid phosphorus
   (e) ethanol solution in water
   (f) liquid sulphur

6. Write the symbol or chemical formula for each of the following substances. Add the state symbol to show whether the substance is a solid, liquid, gas or in solution.
   (a) liquid carbon tetrachloride
   (b) carbon dioxide gas
   (c) oxygen gas
   (d) a solution of sulphur dioxide in water
   (e) solid sulphur
   (f) iodine solid
   (g) silicon oxide solid
   (h) a solution of nitrogen hydride in water

7. Write the chemical formula for each of the following compounds.
   (a) sodium bromide
   (b) potassium chloride
   (c) magnesium chloride
   (d) calcium sulphide
   (e) aluminium oxide
   (f) magnesium oxide
   (g) lithium hydroxide
   (h) potassium sulphate
   (i) caesium nitrate
   (j) potassium carbonate
   (k) strontium sulphate
   (l) ammonium chloride

Credit Level

8. Write the chemical formula for each of the following compounds.
   - (a) calcium hydroxide
   - (b) potassium oxide
   - (c) magnesium nitrite
   - (d) ammonium sulphate
   - (e) lithium carbonate
   - (f) aluminium hydroxide
   - (g) calcium nitrate
   - (h) barium chloride

9. Write the chemical formula for each of the following compounds.
   - (a) lead(II) bromide
   - (b) copper(I) oxide
   - (c) iron(II) chloride
   - (d) nickel(II) sulphate
   - (e) iron(II) carbonate
   - (f) copper(II) hydroxide
   - (g) silver(I) nitrate
   - (h) vanadium(V) oxide

10. Write the symbol or chemical formula for each of the following substances.
    - (a) sodium chloride
    - (b) carbon monoxide
    - (c) magnesium hydroxide
    - (d) hydrogen chloride
    - (e) oxygen
    - (f) iron(III) chloride
    - (g) potassium hydroxide
    - (h) sodium
    - (i) ammonium bromide
    - (j) hydrogen
    - (k) rubidium fluoride
    - (l) sulphur chloride
    - (m) magnesium sulphate
    - (n) ammonium carbonate
    - (o) iron
    - (p) copper(II) oxide
    - (q) sodium sulphide
    - (r) hydrogen fluoride

11. Alums are a group of ionic compounds. Some of them are shown in the table.

Common name	Chemical name	Formula
ammonium alum	aluminium ammonium sulphate	$NH_4Al(SO_4)_2$
chrome alum	chromium(III) potassium sulphate	$KCr(SO_4)_2$
potash alum	**A**	$KAl(SO_4)_2$
ferric alum	ammonium iron(III) sulphate	**B**

   - (a) Write the chemical name for potash alum, **A**.
   - (b) Write the chemical formula for ferric alum, **B**.

Equations
General Level

1. In a chemical reaction, atoms of elements are rearranged. The atoms that are the in the products are from the same elements as those in the reactants.

    (a) Which of the following gases may be obtained by heating copper(II) carbonate ($CuCO_3$)?

        (i)   oxygen   (ii) hydrogen
        (iii) carbon dioxide   (iv) nitrogen

    (b) Which of the following gases may **not** be obtained by heating sodium chromate (Na_2CrO_4)?

        (i)   oxygen   (ii) hydrogen
        (iii) carbon dioxide   (iv) nitrogen

    (c) Which of the following gases may be obtained when calcium reacts with water?

        (i)   oxygen   (ii) hydrogen
        (iii) carbon dioxide   (iv) nitrogen

    (d) Which of the following gases may **not** be obtained when dilute hydrochloric acid (HCl) reacts with calcium sulphate ($CaSO_4$)?

        (i)   oxygen   (ii) hydrogen
        (iii) chlorine   (iv) sulphur dioxide
        (v)   carbon dioxide   (vi) nitrogen

2. Write word equations for each of the following chemical reactions.

    (a) When magnesium metal burns, it reacts with oxygen of the air to form magnesium oxide, a white powder.

    (b) In the Blast furnace, iron is made by reacting iron ore with carbon monoxide gas. Carbon dioxide gas is also produced.

    (c) In our bodies, starch which we get from our food, breaks down to form glucose, which can pass through the walls of our intestines, and water.

    (d) When calcium metal is added to water, a gas is given off and calcium hydroxide solution is formed. When tested with a burning splint, the gas burns with a "pop".

    (e) Copper oxide powder and a gas which turns limewater milky are made when copper carbonate powder is heated.

3. Write a sentence to describe the following reactions. The first one is done for you.

(a) $C(s) + O_2(g) \rightarrow CO_2(g)$

Carbon solid is reacting with oxygen gas to form carbon dioxide gas.

(b) $CO(g) + O_2(g) \rightarrow CO_2(g)$

(c) $C(s) + Cl_2(g) \rightarrow CCl_4(l)$

(d) $H_2(g) + F_2(g) \rightarrow HF(g)$

(e) $SO_2(g) + O_2(g) \rightarrow SO_3(g)$

(f) $CuO(s) + CO(g) \rightarrow Cu(s) + CO_2(g)$

(g) $NH_3(g) \rightarrow N_2(g) + H_2(g)$

(h) $CH_4(g) + O_2(g) \rightarrow CO_2(g) + H_2O(l)$

(i) $HBr(g) \rightarrow H_2(g) + Br_2(l)$

4. Use symbols and formulae to write chemical equations for each of the following reactions.

It is not necessary to balance the equations.

(a) carbon + oxygen → carbon monoxide

(b) sulphur + oxygen → sulphur dioxide

(c) hydrogen chloride → hydrogen + chlorine

(d) nitrogen + oxygen → nitrogen dioxide

(e) phosphorus + chlorine → phosphorus chloride

5. Use symbols and formulae to write chemical equations for each of the following reactions.

It is not necessary to balance the equations.

(a) the burning of hydrogen

(b) the reaction of silicon with chlorine

(c) the burning of ethene (C_2H_4) to form carbon dioxide and water

(d) the formation of hydrogen iodide

(e) the decomposition of nitrogen hydride

6. Use symbols and formulae to write chemical equations for each of the following reactions.

It is not necessary to balance the equations.

(a) calcium + oxygen → calcium oxide

(b) sodium + chlorine → sodium chloride

(c) magnesium + sulphuric acid → magnesium sulphate + hydrogen

(d) magnesium + carbon dioxide → magnesiun oxide + carbon

(e) barium chloride solution + sodium sulphate solution
→ sodium chloride solution + barium sulphate solid

(f) calcium carbonate + hydrochloric acid
→ calcium chloride + carbon dioxide + water

Credit Level

7. Balance each of the following equations.
   (a) $C + O_2 \rightarrow CO_2$
   (b) $P + Cl_2 \rightarrow PCl_3$
   (c) $C + Br_2 \rightarrow CBr_4$
   (d) $C_4H_8 + O_2 \rightarrow CO_2 + H_2O$
   (e) $H_2O_2 \rightarrow H_2O + O_2$

8. Write balanced chemical equations for each of the following reactions.
   (a) carbon monoxide + oxygen $\rightarrow$ carbon dioxide
   (b) hydrogen + chlorine $\rightarrow$ hydrogen chloride
   (c) methane (CH_4) + oxygen $\rightarrow$ carbon dioxide + water
   (d) sulphur dioxide + oxygen $\rightarrow$ sulphur trioxide
   (e) phosphorus + chlorine $\rightarrow$ phosphorus chloride

9. Write balanced chemical equations for each of the following reactions.
   (a) the formation of sulphur trioxide from sulphur dioxide and oxygen
   (b) the combination of carbon with chlorine
   (c) the burning of camping GAZ (C_3H_8) in plenty of air
   (d) the reaction of nitrogen hydride with oxygen to form nitrogen and water
   (e) the combustion of acetylene (C_2H_2) to form carbon dioxide and water

10. Balance each of the following equations.
    (a) $Mg(s) + O_2(g) \rightarrow MgO(s)$
    (b) $Mg(s) + AgNO_3(aq) \rightarrow Mg(NO_3)_2(aq) + Ag(s)$
    (c) $NaOH(aq) + H_2SO_4(aq) \rightarrow Na_2SO_4(aq) + H_2O(l)$
    (d) $AgNO_3(aq) + BaCl_2(aq) \rightarrow Ba(NO_3)_2(aq) + AgCl(s)$
    (e) $Na(s) + H_2O(l) \rightarrow NaOH(aq) + H_2(g)$
    (f) $Al(s) + Cl_2(g) \rightarrow AlCl_3(s)$

11. Write balanced chemical equations for each of the following reactions.
    (a) sodium + oxygen $\rightarrow$ sodium oxide
    (b) magnesium + sulphur dioxide $\rightarrow$ magnesium oxide + sulphur
    (c) calcium + water $\rightarrow$ calcium hydroxide + hydrogen
    (d) calcium oxide + sulphuric acid $\rightarrow$ calcium sulphate + water
    (e) potassium carbonate + hydrochloric acid
        $\rightarrow$ potassium chloride + water + carbon dioxide
    (f) potassium sulphate solution + barium nitrate solution
        $\rightarrow$ potassium nitrate solution + barium sulphate solid

12. Write balanced chemical equations for each of the following reactions.
    (a) sodium hydroxide solution and sulphuric acid
    (b) magnesium oxide and nitric acid
    (c) potassium carbonate solution and hydrochloric acid
    (d) aluminium and sulphuric acid

13. Write balanced chemical equations for each of the following reactions.
    (a) silver(I) nitrate solution and sodium chloride solution
    (b) sodium hydroxide solution and lead(II) chloride solution
    (c) barium chloride solution and sodium sulphate solution
    (d) calcium nitrate solution and potassium carbonate solution
    (e) iron(III) chloride solution and barium hydroxide solution

14. "Superpure" germanium is used in transistors. There are three steps in the process used to purify the germanium.

Step 1.	Germanium combines directly with chlorine.
Step 2.	Water is added to the germanium oxide to form germanium dioxide and hydrogen chloride.
Step 3.	Germanium dioxide reacts with hydrogen to form germanium and water.

    Write balanced chemical equations for each reaction in Steps 1,2 and 3.

15. Some elements exist as diatomic molecules.

    Two such elements, formulae X_2 and Y_2, react together to form a compound.

    An experiment shows that 1 mole of element X reacts exactly with 2 moles of element Y to give 2 moles of compound.

    Use this information to derive the formula for the compound formed between X and Y.

Calculations Based on Equations
Credit Level

1. $$Mg(s) \quad + \quad Cl_2(g) \quad \rightarrow \quad MgCl_2(s)$$
   Calculate the mass of magnesium chloride produced in the reaction of 1.2 g of magnesium with excess chlorine.

2. $$CH_4(g) \quad + \quad 2O_2(g) \quad \rightarrow \quad CO_2(g) \quad + \quad 2H_2O(g)$$
   Calculate the mass of carbon dioxide produced in the reaction of 3.2 g of methane (CH_4) with excess oxygen.

3. $$4Na(s) \quad + \quad O_2(g) \quad \rightarrow \quad 2Na_2O(s)$$
   Calculate the mass of sodium oxide produced in the reaction of 2.3 g of sodium with excess oxygen.

4. $$N_2(g) \quad + \quad 3H_2(g) \quad \rightarrow \quad 2NH_3(g)$$
   Calculate the mass of hydrogen required to react with 56 g of nitrogen.

5. $$4Al(s) \quad + \quad 3O_2(g) \quad \rightarrow \quad 2Al_2O_3(s)$$
   Calculate the mass of oxygen required to react with 2.7 g of aluminium.

6. $$Mg(s) \quad + \quad CuSO_4(aq) \quad \rightarrow \quad MgSO_4(aq) \quad + \quad Cu(s)$$
   Calculate the mass of copper produced in the reaction of 1.2 g of magnesium with excess copper(II) sulphate.

7. As a result of recycling, an industrial plant converts 7.7×10^4 kg of hydrogen to ammonia each day.
   $$N_2(g) \quad + \quad 3H_2(g) \quad \rightarrow \quad 2NH_3(g)$$
   Calculate the mass of ammonia which is produced each day.

8. Ammonium sulphate is a fertiliser. The compound can be produced by the reaction of ammonia with sulphuric acid.
   $$2NH_3(g) \quad + \quad H_2SO_4(aq) \quad \rightarrow \quad (NH_4)_2SO_4$$
   Calculate the mass of ammonium sulphate which could be produced from 170 kg of ammonia.

9. Ammonia can be formed by adding water to magnesium nitride.
   $$Mg_3N_2(s) + 6H_2O \,(l) \quad \rightarrow \quad 3Mg(OH)_2(s) + \; 2NH_3(g)$$
   Calculate the mass of ammonia produced when 30 g of magnesium nitride are added to excess water.

10. A power station produces sulphur dioxide, an atmospheric pollutant.
    The sulphur dioxide can be removed by reaction with limestone (calcium carbonate).
    $$CaCO_3 \quad + \quad SO_2 \quad \rightarrow \quad CaSO_3 \quad + \quad CO_2$$
    Calculate the mass of calcium carbonate required to remove completely 580 tonnes of sulphur dioxide.

11. The monomer for polythene can be produced from ethanol.

| ethanol | | ethene | | water |

Calculate the maximum mass of ethene which can be produced from 6900 kg of ethanol.

12. Nitrogen is used to fill the air-bags which protect people in car crashes.
    It is produced when sodium azide (NaN_3) decomposes rapidly.

$$2NaN_3(s) \rightarrow 2Na(s) + 3N_2(g)$$

A driver's air-bag contains 60 g of sodium azide.

Calculate the mass of nitrogen gas which would be produced.

13. Octane burns in a plentiful supply of air to produce carbon dioxide and water.

$$C_8H_{18}(l) + 12\tfrac{1}{2}O_2(g) \rightarrow 8CO_2(g) + 9H_2O(g)$$

Calculate the mass of carbon dioxide produced by the burning of 57 tonnes of octane.